ART
in
QUESTION

LONDON LECTURES IN
CONTEMPORARY CHRISTIANITY, 1984

The London Lectures in Contemporary Christianity were founded in 1974. Their purpose is to develop biblical Christian thinking on the issues of the day. They are delivered annually, in association with the London Institute for Contemporary Christianity, which is now located in St Peter's Church, Vere Street, London W1. Chairman of the Lectures Committee is John Stott.

*Other titles in the London Lectures series published by
Marshall Pickering*

The Year 2000 AD, *ed. John Stott*
Free to be Different:
Varieties of Human Behaviour, *ed. John Stott*
The Good of the People, *ed. John Gladwin*

ART
in
QUESTION

LONDON LECTURES IN
CONTEMPORARY CHRISTIANITY, 1984

edited
by
Tim Dean and David Porter

Marshall Pickering

Marshall Morgan and Scott
Marshall Pickering
3 Beggarwood Lane, Basingstoke, Hants RG23 7LP, UK

Copyright © 1987 Tim Dean and David Porter
First published in 1987 by Marshall Morgan and Scott Publications Ltd
Part of the Marshall Pickering Holdings Group
A subsidiary of the Zondervan Corporation

Neither the Council of the London Institute nor the London
Lectures Committee necessarily endorses all the views that
the lecturers express.
ISBN 0–551–01321–4

Text set in Linotron Plantin
by Input Typesetting Ltd, London
Printed in Great Britain by
Camelot Press Ltd, Shirley, Southampton

Contents

List of Contributors

Dr Graham Birtwistle, formerly senior lecturer in art history at Leicester Polytechnic 1964–70, is now lecturing at the Free University of Amsterdam. His book *Living Art: Asger Jorn's comprehensive theory of art between Helhesten and Cobra (1946–1949)* was published in 1986 (Reflex, Utrecht).

William Edgar studied music and ethnomusicology at Harvard and Columbia universities, and theology in Philadelphia and Geneva. He is the former editor of *Genesis* magazine, and is now professor of apologetics at the Faculté Libre de Théologie Réformée, Aix-en-Provence, France. His book, *Taking Note of Music* was published in 1986 (SPCK/Third Way Books).

Ruth Etchells is Principal of St John's College with Cranmer Hall, University of Durham, and teacher in the English and theology departments of the University. Her most recent book is *A Model of Making* (Marshalls, 1983).

David Porter is an author and editor. He has published three collections of poetry. His play *Bad Angel* was produced by Upstream Theatre Company. His most recent book is *Children at Risk* (Kingsway, 1986).

Peter Smith was West Midlands Arts' Fine Art Fellow 1977–9, and is now Head of Art at the Kingston College of Further Education. He has exhibited his work in the West Midlands, London and Amsterdam. He is a member of the Society of Wood Engravers.

Murray Watts is an author and playwright, much of whose career has been spent with Riding Lights Theatre Company, of which he was a co-founder. His most recent book is *Christianity and the Theatre* (Handsel Press, 1986).

Editors' Introduction

The London Lectures in Contemporary Christianity were founded in 1974 as an annual lecture series intended to promote Christian thought about contemporary issues. The series which is contained in the present book, *Art in Question*, addressed a number of related questions. What are the contemporary arts telling us about the world in which we live? What do they tell us about ourselves? What responsibilities come with our God-given capacity to create?

That such questions should be thought to merit an extended series of public lectures in a prominent evangelical venue is of itself significant. It is only in recent years that the arts have been considered by evangelical Christians as justifiable areas to be involved in, at least for purposes other than evangelism. Certainly these lectures cannot be accused of mere utilitarianism, as even a cursory glance will show.

The lectures look backward as well as forward. All the lecturers have been active in the arts in the period following the mid-sixties, when a resurgence of evangelical interest in the arts took place. In Britain it was largely prompted by the early lectures of Hans Rookmaaker in 1968, the beginning of systematic co-ordination of Christians in the Arts Colleges within UCCF, the establishment of the Arts Centre Group and the beginning of English L'Abri. But it would be quite wrong to say that this resurgence represented something new and revolutionary. Christian writing on the arts had been represented well before the sixties by C. S. Lewis, J. R. R. Tolkien, Charles William, G. K. Chesterton, Dorothy L. Sayers and many others.

Yet something new *was* happening in the late sixties.

It was, we suggest, firstly a natural shift in evangelical thinking. When one looks at books published, magazines founded, and popular Christian debate, it is slightly simplistic (but still valid) to see in the period from the end of World War II to the late sixties a particular emphasis on Christianity and science; from the mid-sixties to the mid-seventies, an emphasis on Christianity and the arts: and from the mid-seventies to the present, an emphasis on Christianity and social and political issues such as liberation theology, sociology, the role of women, war and peace, and similar issues.

It was a shift that was characterized by several significant factors.

It was *a Christian response to a perceived need*. The late sixties were a period of prolific artistic experimentation, and of statement through art. Messages both explicit and implicit were carried by rock music, absurd theatre, modern art, sculpture and architecture, and literature, besides the mainstream arts. In the late sixties, several Christian organizations and individuals began to teach that the Bible did in fact contain valid answers to the questions being posed in the arts, and that faith in, and a relationship with, Jesus Christ was not only intellectually credible but was also a solid foundation for creativity and working in the arts.

Moreover, it was *a response of the whole person*. It transcended solely pietistic responses. Those Christians who felt called to practise and critique the arts included many who had thought through their own positions long and carefully. They included academics like Hans Rookmaaker, Calvin Seerveld and Nicholas Wolterstorff; Francis Schaeffer, Os Guiness, the group influenced by Hermann Dooyerweerd, and several other apologists; and a large number of practising artists and art students who went on to make names for themselves in the secular world and to involve themselves in the secular debate. Few in the sixties and seventies described their call, if they described it at all, as one to make altar-cloths or tracts.

Finally, it was – as we have implied – *a unique blend of theory and practice*. The conferences of the period included art theorists and artists, and each, by and large, was willing to learn from the other.

In many ways, the resurgence of interest in the arts at that time had something of the flavour of the mediaeval scholars, who toured Europe with their pupils in train. Hans Rookmaaker, for example, provoked great affection and respect in those who learned from him. It is a flavour which we hope the present volume reflects, containing as it does contributions from those who assess the arts and those who practise them.

These lectures, given in the mid-eighties, have perhaps a particular significance. The sixties were a revolutionary period; revolution of many kinds was in the very air one breathed. The Christian resurgence of interest in the arts shared the same climate, and for Christians there was a rediscovery of the transformational ethic of their faith. The whole of society and human culture should be changed, not only individual lives. Those involved wanted not merely to use the arts, but to change them; and the same can be said of all culturally relevant art movements that have had credibility.

Art in Question has as its reference that rich period in Christian cultural involvement, but Christianity and art did not cease to be a live issue in the mid-seventies. On the contrary, today there are increasing numbers of Christian art students and of Christians actively involved in the arts, and also there is an increasing Christian representation in teachers of art and those who write about it.

This series of lectures consequently in part fulfils the purposes of a stock-taking (notably in Graham Birtwistle's introductory essay), and also in part fulfils the purposes of an agenda.

The contributors reflect the diversity of the subject and of the Christian artistic community.

Graham Birtwistle presents an overview of art, providing some definitions of the essential concept, examining some published discussions of art and offering some evaluation of the role of art theory in society.

William Edgar tackles the task of developing criteria for art. How do we distinguish between good and bad art? He approaches this problem by way of the difficult area of rock music, assessing various critiques by Christians and proposing nothing less than the redemption of rock culture.

Ruth Etchells considers modern literature and distinguishes several strands within it which indicate various directions being followed. Appropriately, in vew of her chosen title, she presents her findings as a challenge to the reader; how, as Christians, do we – and should we – read books?

David Porter contributes an observer's view of television and video, assessing both as social phenomena and also providing a critique on several levels.

Murray Watts writes as a playwright, and as a practitioner of theatre – an area of the arts traditionally treated with extreme reservation by evangelical Christians. He provides an analysis of contemporary theatre, and links it with an illuminating discussion of the pressures and challenges faced by Christians working in it.

Peter Smith writes as a painter, and talks about his struggle to come to terms with his work and with our expectations of it. His closing challenge to Christian artists to see their work as primarily 'honest labour', useful in revealing the potential of creation, has added force, coming as it does after his rigorous examination of that task on the aesthetic and theological levels.

Each lecturer has revised the original lecture for publication in this book, with the exception of Ruth Etchells, whose revision was cut short by illness and completed by the editors.

Murray Watts was one of the original team of lecturers, but was obliged to withdraw through personal circumstances; his chapter in this book is adapted by the editors from material which was to have been used in his lecture, and which is now available in a much expanded form as a book published by Handsel Press, under the title *Christianity and the Theatre*. Alby James, director of Temba Theatre Company, was invited to take Murray's place in the lecture series. His lecture was much appreciated, but owing to professional pressures a revised version was not available for inclusion in the present book.

Tim Dean and David Porter
Editors

Tim Dean is editor of Third Way *magazine, did postgraduate film studies at University College London, and worked in broadcasting. He played a large part in the planning of the lecture series. David Porter was one of the six lecturers.*

Art and the Arts

by Graham Birtwistle

An introductory chapter to a published book on 'Art and the Arts' might reasonably be expected to go further than ordinary conversation can in providing a definition of art and its values. However, I shall be approaching the subject in a somewhat indirect, even evasive way; I shall be suggesting, in fact, that the term 'art' is one that can be of greater use when it remains as a term-of-convenience then when it is forged into a tightly defined theoretical concept. In explaining why I am adopting this course, I also want to try to turn what appears to be a negative standpoint into a positive one.

The words 'art' and 'artist' are in regular use. Most of us are ready to expound without much provocation on what we like and what we don't like, on what is and what isn't art, and on who deserves the title 'artist' and who doesn't. There is indeed something about art which seems to invite qualitative evaluation. In talking about works of art we constantly use evaluative terms such as 'good', 'beautiful', and 'powerful' – or their opposites – while even art historians and theorists, who might take pains to avoid such terminology in their professional work, can be caught using it after-hours when their word-processors have been turned off. Personal taste plays an undeniable role in all this, but the very fact that we discuss and write about art so much shows that we are concerned to be more than individual islands of taste. Here, however, we strike a very real problem: not only are particular values in art equivocal, but so is the concept of 'art' itself.

'Art' has a variety of meanings and implications which reveal themselves in ordinary conversation as switches of emphasis or even contradictions. Do we mean by 'art' just painting and sculpture? Sometimes we do, but an art historian also studies architecture, church silver and a host of other objects, while an 'arts programme' on television or an 'arts section' of the newspaper usually includes such disciplines as film, literature, music, theatre and ballet. According to its context, 'art' is sometimes meant in a narrower, sometimes in a wider sense; sometimes the word is used exclusively, sometimes popularly. We have become adept at slipping from one meaning over into another, but as soon as discussion about art becomes heated, the different implications of the word seem to sharpen into topics of great controversy and the conversation can take on a Babel-like aspect.

One side of this has to do with the relation of past and present. In our museums we house works from the past while at the same time adding to them the works we estimate to be of importance from the present. The same principle holds for the non-visual arts; we continue to perform music and drama and read books written in the course of the centuries, as well of those of today. For most of us, our record collections, our bookshelves, and the pictures on our walls represent a personal museum. Even our discussions about art can have this museum-like quality; we frequently flit between various old and new notions, often without realizing that we are doing it.

In earlier ages a mingling of the old and the new always marked attitudes to art, but nowadays the scale and complexity of this question is difficult to take in. Compared with a century ago, vastly more works, culled from our own and other traditions, are presented to us as art and made accessible in museums, performances, and, not least, in the pages of countless books and magazines. And we, the interested public, have increased vastly in numbers too; educated, curious and fashionable, we have become tourists of a world history of the arts; and – in tune with our times – are ever ready to express an opinion about what we see, hear and read. But we rarely stop to think that our ideas on art, like the works themselves, also come from a variety of sources. Discussions of art, even on a specialized level, are frequently a jumble of arguments which have been formed and rehearsed earlier in history.

A good deal of the difficulty we have today in defining art can be traced to the fact that our 'museum' of ideas about art is less clearly visible to us than the museums in which we actually house it. The historical process has been one of selection and transformation, and not simply of retention. Some values and priorities, and even some arts, have more or less vanished or changed in status. For example, we are not accustomed nowadays to review the speeches of our politicians, the lectures of our teachers, or the sermons of our ministers of religion, in the light of one of the foundational arts of our western tradition: that of rhetoric. On the other hand, music has certainly grown in status during the past two centuries and some would even argue that it is the first among all the arts.

During the past hundred years or so shifts in evaluation have also brought recognition as art for categories which were earlier regarded as less than art: works from tribal cultures and folk arts, for example. Many of these changes have ridden in on the wave of a modernism which has found, in non-western and non-academic cultural expressions, the means to assert values deemed more dynamic and authentic than those of the western 'classical' tradition.

The controversies have been heated, and few changes have occurred without entrenched resistance. But once the dust has settled, the general pattern which emerges is that of an expansion and diversification of our understanding of what art can be; so that a conservative theologian like Francis Schaeffer could write in 1973 what a half-century earlier only a handful of avant-garde artists and connoisseurs were saying:

> When I look at the pre-Columbian silver or African masks or ancient Chinese bronzes, not only do I see them as works of art but I see them as expressions of the nature and character of humanity. As a man, in a certain way they are myself . . . [1]

This same process is continuing at the present day, and two 'signs of the times' must suffice to indicate the direction in which I am thinking. In the first place, I have noted a tendency in recent years for leading newspapers in both Britain and Holland to present a more 'democratic' arts page, integrating reviews of popular music and culture with the more established or 'serious' arts. Secondly, in Anthony Burgess's published selection of the best novels since 1939, the inclusion of thrillers by writers such as Raymond Chandler and Ian Fleming, and the apologetics presented for them, showed that Burgess was quite conscious of challenging literary hierarchies.[2]

His point was not that we should lower our standards, but rather the opposite: we should look for quality but be prepared to find it outside an official élite. Though in themselves apparently insignificant, such shifts in evaluation (multiplied in their effect by similiar examples in other fields), are continuing to alter the boundaries of what is understood as art. This had only been possible as stricter, more exclusive definitions have been relaxed, but the net effect need not be a loss of values. The challenge is now, I would suggest, to try to discern the values appropriate and *specific* to the many activities, professions and products which we group together – loosely and plurally – as 'the arts'.

The situation we face is complex. On the one hand, the trend towards extending and diversifying the concept of art seems the dominant historical one; while on the other, our actual discussions and evaluations often persist in keeping more narrow and limiting notions alive. Some ten years ago I attended a symposium in Amsterdam on photography, to which some of the best-known American and European photographers were invited. What struck me was that they seemed obsessed by the problem that photography was insufficiently recognized as 'Art' and as directly comparable with painting, a 'problem' which seemed to me then, as now, both anachronistic and actually distracting from the real issues at hand. Certainly, painting is an older tradition in providing visual images and its history and potential can offer much food for thought to a photographer. But while they overlap on some points, painting and photography diverge on others, and photography has its own particular way of working. The only explanation for 'the problem' was, in fact, that a surplus-value was being attributed to painting as an 'Art' and that photographers were desirous of annexing this special status (and, perhaps, a corresponding economic value?) to their own profession.

The problem of Art (with a capital A) still haunts us today. The idea that there is a higher, finer, non-commercial, non-utilitarian, mystical and inspired – and, curiously enough, when one is established, more expensive – category which renders some arts 'Real Art' and others mere art (or less) still pervades our expectations. In some respects it is the problem which Nicholas Wolterstorff has dealt with in sociological terms in his book *Art in Action*, distinguishing our society's institution of 'high art' (the art of the gallery-, concert-, theatre-going cultural élite) from 'popular art' and 'art of the tribe' (art and design used by everyone in a given society).[3] Wolterstorff, professor of philosophy at Calvin College in the United States, steers an astute course round the problem. In emphasizing that art can have many purposes he removes from 'high art' any prerogative to be the one and only way in which art and its values are to be defined. Moreover, he writes,

> The Christian must resist the claims of ultimacy which repeatedly erupt for our institution of high art. Art does not provide us with the meaning of human existence. The gospel of Jesus Christ does that. (p.196)

But Wolterstorff is also careful not to throw out the proverbial baby with the bathwater:

> Like almost everything else in our history, the status of our institution of high art is ambivalent. Our response to it must be a No *and* a Yes. From the resources of the institution has come forth a flood of great works which together have enriched and deepened our lives immeasurably. (p.193)

What Wolterstorff advocates is a critical and relativizing attitude to 'high art', so that we can see art in a wider perspective and be 'freed to act understandingly and appreciatively toward otherwise overlooked or inscrutable parts of our own artistic tradition' (p.192). Wolterstorff's approach does not catch all the nuances of the problem, and I suspect that a rigid belief in 'high art' may, paradoxically enough, even have become more a popular notion than one characteristic of cultural leaders (like Wolterstorff himself!) in our day. But his book provides a wealth of argument and illustrations for the plurality of artistic purposes and functions in our society.

In its relativization of 'high art' Wolterstorff's approach bears a certain similarity to the course already set by two of the most influential Christian theorists of the past decades, H. R. Rookmaaker and Francis Schaeffer. In their work for L'Abri Fellowship (which the Schaeffer family founded) and in their publications and lectures (Rookmaaker was also professor of the history of art at the Free University of Amsterdam) they stimulated and guided a

generation of Christian artists representative of the whole spectrum
of the arts.

When H. R. Rookmaaker published his *Modern Art and the Death
of a Culture* some fifteen years ago, no-one could have missed the
impact of his biblical Christian critique. But it is salutary to
remember that Rookmaaker's view of art was at least as 'democratic'
as the one I am advocating here, taking in older traditions in art as
well as modern art and weaving into his argument substantial
elements from popular music and culture. Though explicitly a Christian critique of modernism, Rookmaaker's book was contemporary
enough to look for significance in art forms which were by no means
exclusively 'Art', a factor which made his book interesting to (for
example) sociologists who did not necessarily share his Christian
standpoint. But Rookmaaker's view of a broad spectrum of the arts
was more than simply an attunement to a contemporary trend; it
had a specific thrust as a product of his Christian thinking; it
contained a diatribe against too narrow and exclusive a concept of
'Art':

> Perhaps one of the main problems of art today has been the result
> of giving art the wrong function. Formerly art was 'an art', just
> as we speak of arts and crafts. Art as a higher function of
> mankind, the work of the inspired lofty artist, comparable to that
> of the poet and prophet, was the outcome of the Renaissance with
> its neo-platonic way of thinking. . . . Art became Art with a
> capital A, a high, exalted, more humanist than human endeavour.
> Yet precisely in that pseudo-religious function it became almost
> superfluous, something aside from reality and life, a luxury – fine,
> refined, but useless.[4]

Rookmaaker's account of art as simply 'an art' and his critique of
a pseudo-religious belief in Art was, to my mind, a relevant Christian
message for his time. But I think that the broad, democratic view
of the arts he was proposing was something new. Like the arts-and-
crafts theories of the nineteenth century it was shaped in part by
reference to earlier times. But, rather than the rediscovery of something which had once existed, it was a modern formulation, rooted
more in Rookmaaker's own ideals than in historical documentation.
And, as with Wolterstorff's 'No and Yes' to the institution of 'high

art' in society, I think that Rookmaaker's theory was consonant with a Christian standpoint, firstly in its concern to free attitudes to art from a troublesome mysticism and even idolatory (listen to Isaiah 44), and secondly in its regard for the variety and potency of God's cultural mandate for mankind.

Here we can note what is at first sight a curious characteristic in the writings of Rookmaaker, and also those of his close colleague Francis Schaeffer. Where we expect them to define art they tend not to. While they discuss a variety of arts, high and low, popular and esoteric, at the point at which we might expect a specific theory of art they tend to provide, instead, a more general theory of culture or creativity:

> Art is not a religion, nor an activity relegated to a chosen few, nor a mere worldly, superfluous affair. None of these views of art does justice to the creativity with which God has endowed man. It is the ability to make something beautiful (as well as useful), just as God made the world beautiful and said, 'It is good.'[5]

Put bluntly, Rookmaaker and Schaeffer both seem to have taken art in all its diverse guises as the expression of a fundamental creativity, without the intervention of an intermediary definition of art. Though on this, as on other points, their methods are open to theoretical critique, in practice I think the course they set was not without a certain wisdom and was an implicit recognition of the point I raised earlier: that the arts as we know them are too diverse in character and function to admit of definition under one tight formula. In grounding the arts in a more general biblically-based theory of culture or creativity they gave both direction and freedom of movement to these loosely-allied professions. It made good Christian sense, I think, to be emphatic about the basic principles on which our human culture is based, to be open as regards the diversity of arts which form our cultural life, and to be wary of offering a prescriptive definition of art which intervenes between the principles and their multi-facted outworking.

Here, however, it must be noted that even the formulation of basic biblical principles can be controversial. The cultural mandate and a charter for creativity are not necessarily the same thing, and it is on this point that Calvin Seerveld, professor of aesthetics at the Institute for Christian Studies in Toronto, diverges from theorists like Rookmaaker and Schaeffer:

> Comparisons between God as capital A Creator Artist and man as small, image-of-God creator artist are only speculative and misleading. To turn analysis of 'what now is human artistic activity?' into a theo-logical discussion on the unique 'creativity' of God is no help at all in determining the nature and place of art on earth. Such a would-be christian approach is often caught in the age-old trap of *analogia entis*. Once you work in that problematics you have to be a scholastic casuist to escape the heresy of mysticism, deism or a covert blasphemy.[6]

That this is a particularly controversial issue can be seen from recent correspondence in the magazine *Third Way*.[7] I would readily agree that many 'image-of-God' formulations, including some used by Rookmaaker and Schaeffer, are theologically somewhat carefree, but I also regard the other extreme, as represented by Seerveld and some of his students, as pedantic. While it is clear that 'creation' in the Bible is attributed only to God, many anthropomorphizing terms overlap with it – 'work', 'hands', 'making', 'fashioning', for example (Gen. 2.1–3; Isa. 45.9–13; John 1, 3) – and to my mind there is room enough in this biblical language to understand what Schaeffer was after when he wrote of the arts that 'the word *create* is appropriate, for it suggests that what man does with what is already there is to make something new. Something that was not there before . . .'[8]

The cultural mandate, with its starting-point in God's command to fill the earth and subdue it, may be regarded as an issue on which Christian theorists have exhibited a more general agreement. In his usual pungent terms Calvin Seerveld has put it this way:

> Culture is not optional. Formative culturing of creation is intrinsic to human nature, put there purposely – God knows why . . . the creation of God is unfinished, waiting historically to be used; its variegated meanings are waiting there to be unleased in a new chorus of praise for the Lord. This is our human calling.[9]

Such a view is anchored in the first chapters of Genesis and implies, too, that the rest of the Bible in all its dimensions will be relevant to the outworking in history of this calling.

The cultural mandate is full of potential, but unspecific. In being more specific, in focusing on works of art and attitudes of art, we are confronted by the historical nature of our response to the cultural mandate, both in the variety which makes up the whole array and in the historical limitations to which each of us is subject. Theories of art are themselves responses in history, and no more and no less than that; their value should be healthily relativized rather than absolutized. The Christian books on art which we have on our shelves are all of them datable and reflect the context – cultural, theological, philosophical – in which they were written. Moreover, they also reflect the personal taste and preferences of their authors, something which can be more obvious to the reader than to the writer!

Such factors do not invalidate the discussion of the arts or the particular theories advanced. Rather, they are intrinsic to the living and necessarily subjective process of action, reaction and renewal, which must always mark our cultural life.

For example, in the sixties and early seventies I moved in circles in which a taste for natural materials predominated: plastic was out! Such an attitude was motivated Christianly, and was also in tune with a somewhat primitivistic tendency in the taste and ideas of those years. That standpoint was not invalidated but certainly historically relativized when a later swing in taste made it clear that artistic excellence could also reside in products made of artificial materials: plastic was in! Alternations and discoveries of potential serve to localize the value of the rules and principles we invent for our art and taste, and though a culture of throwaway consumption can bring an unnatural frenzy to the inherent changeability of the arts, the opposite danger – the desire to freeze history and perpetuate our styles and their values – can be just as much of a menace.

It is therefore with an eye to this historical diversity – and, not least, with an eye to the diversity of professions represented in this present book – that I regard certain leading questions as unanswerable or inappropriate. Given the variety – from painters to media-people to jazz musicians – it strikes me as singularly unhelpful even to try to decide if one of them is more truly, more typically an artist

than another, or, conversely, if there is one special aesthetic factor –
beauty, fittingness, symbolic richness, or metaphoric intensity? –
which best and most centrally defines what is common to all of their
works. Here I must apologize to some of my colleagues for appearing
to pass so lightly over their detailed and stimulating accounts of just
such problems, but now that I am beginning to fly my colours more
clearly from the mast I want to emphasize that my approach is that
of an art historian, not that of a philosopher or an artist. Both the
latter may have their good reasons for taking a more direct or
exclusive course in defining their conception of art.

To my historian's mind, there is no one single art theory which
serves as a basis for all that we today call 'the arts'. All the theories
of art and aesthetics which I have come across to date have a more
limitative character than the actual spectrum of the arts which we
have, in practice, accepted. Explicitly or by default such theories
are better attuned to some arts than to others. 'The arts', as a term,
indicates no more than a loose alliance of professions which may or
may not share working experiences and problems. Sir John
Betjeman apart, the poet may not have too much in common with
the architect, or the textile designer with the classical guitarist, and
in the academic world the studies of literature and the visual arts –
and even the historical specializations within each of these fields –
are pursued in quite characteristic, separate ways. I am labouring
this point in order to draw an experimental, though serious,
conclusion; that we might relax the demand to define art in any
exclusive sense strikes me as one of the more interesting possibilities
open to us in the late twentieth century.

What I propose, then, in place of an attempt at a unifying, definition
of art, is a general recognition of our cultural task and our possibilities and responsibilities under God on his earth; and then a close
focus on the specific occupations and situations which we face. I
think it is still relevant as Christians to refuse a bogus cultural
mandate, one that would interpose itself as an artistic direction and
goal for our lives and thereby take over as a pseudo-religious principle underlying our endeavours.

Biblically, Christians are enjoined to see themselves as members
of one body of which the head is Christ. If theologians will permit

me, I think there are lessons to be learned from this image of the Church which extend beyond its direct application. As fingers and toes we are different but organically related and inter-dependent, and above all humbly aware of the fact that no one of us human beings is the head. Transposed to our discussion of the arts I would venture to say that we perhaps yet need to realize more fully that no one member of the body may appropriate exclusivity and a status which renders others undervalued and under-rewarded.

Exclusive theories of a higher kind of Art sometimes come dangerously close to assuming not only status but the prerogative of headship; and if I am trying – perhaps too provocatively – to dismantle some of our ideas about the special nature of Art, this is one of the factors I have in view. It may be that here what I have termed a 'democratic' tendency in the arts finds a more directly biblical foundation.

Though it may at first sight appear so, I am not at all interested in debunking what we call the 'fine arts', nor am I advocating any relaxation of the demand for excellence in what we do. Behind the question 'Is it Art?' lies the quite justifiable hope that excellence may be found and demonstrated. What am I doing is refracting that call for excellence into a whole range of questions concerning a great variety of artistic endeavours. Instead of asking 'Is it Art?' I would prefer to ask: 'Is it a good painting?' or 'Is it a well-designed telephone?' Such questions turn our attention to the criteria relevant to paintings or telephones, and in both areas we may hope that something of a high grade may be achieved.

Of course, I am fully aware that the question of a hierarchical order lurks behind this discussion of value: is not painting itself somehow higher, more truly 'Art', than designing a telephone? Here, as with Wolterstorff's ambivalent 'No and Yes' to high art, we must be careful how we tread. In one sense, painting may be seen as a more complex and intensified way of imaging the thought-world of the artist than designing. I know painters who feel very conscious of this distinction. Painting would seem to be less tied to the practical and ephemeral demands of life than designing and thus – like pure science as opposed to technology, academic writing as opposed to journalism, or theology as opposed to preaching – it would seem to be more durable, more highly refined.

However, I am not sure that any of the distinctions we have touched on above are best expressed hierarchically. In fact I suspect that it is a Christian, rather than a humanist or any other kind of insight, to suggest that all our tasks are inter-related and inter-dependant and that it is spiritually and socially responsible to see them as such. Like Wolterstorff, I would want to maintain the value of works produced in the name of 'high art' while at the same time turning to examine 'the paths opened up to us by being liberated from its grip on our thought and practice.'[10]

Since, apart from this exhortation, I have refrained from laying an art-theoretical basis for my colleagues who work in the arts, it is logical that I, like the reader, am now curious to see what are the specific situations they have been facing and what are the responses they as Christians have brought to them. This expectation is, in fact, the 'hidden theory' of my essay. I am convinced that the role of the theoretician – in this case the art historian – is, like that of other members of the body, limited. It is perhaps a fault of our Christian community that leadership is often assumed to reside in the work of theoretical definition. To my mind this need not be so, and it is a particular virtue of the arts that they present us with the richness of our humanity in other than a theoretical form.

In this respect, it is important that we neither undervalue nor overvalue the role of theory in the arts. While a study of seventeenth-century ideas and art theory may help us to understand Rembrandt better, no amount of such knowledge could lead us to surmise, let alone predict, the actual qualities to be found in his paintings – if we had never seen them. Rembrandts are not painted theories, but they do arouse questions which can best be discussed and dealt with theoretically.

In our contemporary situation theory is (just like the arts themselves) multi-functional. A number of years ago it was the task of some Christian theorists to assume leadership in actually urging Christian artists to see their vocation as a worthy one and in opening the eyes of a broad Christian public to the valuable role of the artists among them. That kind of leadership is perhaps not so necessary now, since it has clearly borne its fruits. Today there is a small army of Christians, diversely talented and active in many countries, whose work already represents years of accumulated expertise and experience in the arts. It is now time to take stock of what has been done, of what problems have been faced and of what failures and successes have been booked. Now, if the theorist has a certain function of leadership it is perhaps best to see him in the role of a chairman who, though invested with the authority to limit loquaciousness, succeeds in his task when he manages to elicit and orchestrate the experiences which the members of the meeting have to relate.

Notes

1. F. A. Schaeffer, *Art and the Bible*, Downers Grove, Ill., 1973, p.35.
2. *Sunday Times Review*, 12–2–1984, pp.33–4.
3. N. Wolterstorff, *Art in Action*, Grand Rapids, Mi., 1980, p. 22.
4. H. R. Rookmaaker, *Modern Art and the Death of a Culture*, London, 1970, pp.230–1.
5. H. R. Rookmaaker, *The Creative Gift*, Westchester, Ill., 1981, p.113. See also F. A. Schaeffer, op. cit., pp.33–5.
6. C. G. Seerveld, *Rainbows for the Fallen World*, Toronto, 1980, p.26.
7. Adrienne Chaplin, 'Creative Idealism', *Third Way*, Dec. 1985, pp. 18–21; and letters by R. Kojecky and A. Chaplin in the subsequent February and April 1986 numbers.
8 F. A. Schaeffer, op. cit., p.35.
9. C. G. Seerveld, op. cit., pp.24–5.
10. N. Wolterstorff, op. cit., p.192.

The Message of Rock Music

by William Edgar

As people find their seats, fasten their safety belts and wait for take-off, music with a moderate rock beat is piped in over the plane's system. The ladies pushing their carts around the aisles of the corner supermarket hardly hear the muffled sounds of the wall-to-wall disco music that helps them forget the high prices. Thumbing through the magazine rack at the railroad station news-stand, the young man looks through scores of rock-related journals until he finds just the one he wants, the one with all the posters. Just home from school, the children turn on the TV set, hoping to catch a few video-clips before getting down to their homework.

Who could have predicted from its modest origins in the southern United States in the 1950s that rock 'n' roll would become the major sound track of the latter part of the century? It is, of course, a major industry whose markets are all over the world. In 1985, Britain earned $1.5 billion from exports of its pop music, more than for tobacco, sugar, clothing and steel.

The detailed conditions of this music's production distribution and impact are often poorly understood, partly because it is all so vast. Arguments about the nature of rock, its influence on modern life, its 'message' are all the more difficult to manage in that definitions are elusive. What qualifies as rock? Pink Floyd's synthesized sound poems would seem to have no kinship with the Ramone's stripped-down punk music. George Clinton is miles away from Sade and David Bowie. Still, it seems legitimate to speak of 'rock'. As a cultural force, in the midst of the variety, there is a centre of gravity.

Rock 'n' roll is more than a musical form. There are identifiable traits, though. The 12– or 16–bar shape, a shuffle-bass, accents off the beat, electric guitars, blues style, etc. – these ingredients help us to say 'this is rock', or 'this is not rock'. But there is more than a musical genre. There is a certain ambiance. In 30 years of its existence, rock 'n' roll has never been quite content merely to entertain. Lyrics may be banal ('Funny how love is . . .'), ironic ('Yesterday's preacher, today's bikini beacher'), or sentimental ('I chase the bright elusive butterfly of love'). Yet there is a greater distance between Elvis Presley and Frank Sinatra then between Sinatra and Al Bowley. This is partly because the roots of rock 'n' roll are in folk art rather than show business. Rock was a liberating factor for young people in the post-war era. It seemed to be more honest, at least to what people felt about their bodies. Elvis' girations, which look mild enough today, challenged not only the modesty and restraint of commercial popular music, but its saccharine sentimentality as well.

The term rock is a synonym for 'swing' in black American culture. To swing is to play in a fluid rhythm, often achieved by subtly accentuating the off-beat over a regular pulse. It is more of a feeling to be learned than a mechanically appropriated method. A number of early jazz song titles used the word. Duke Ellington's *Rockin' in Rhythm* is one example. In the vocal part of Chick Webb's *Rock It for Me*, Ella Fitzgerald sings, 'You ought to satisfy my soul with rock and roll'. These songs came out of the 1930s, well before the rock era. Rhythm and blues musician Louis Jordan played rock music in the 1940s. Thus, the pre-history of modern rock can be traced to black American roots. Attention must be drawn especially to the realism of the blues, whose lyrics, unlike Broadway show music, were directed to earthly, tangible realities, such as finding or losing a lover, getting a job, hypocritical religion, money, drink.

The early pioneers of rock, Elvis Presley, Bill Haley, Buddy Holly, and so on, borrowed heavily from the black tradition. Disc jockeys like Alan Freed (who is wrongly credited with the invention of the term rock and roll) began playing black music on white stations in Cleveland in 1951. And while so much of the new, white rock of the 1950s sounds bland and commercial, compared to Frank Sinatra it was a breath of fresh air. The injection of the blues element, coupled with Alan Freed's disc jockey talking style, made for the beginnings of a new musical culture.

The power of rock music is not easily reduced to one thing,

however. The realism of the blues had an impact on white culture in the 1950s because there was a need among the affluent whites. Part of that need was the emptiness of the materialistic post-war generation. Rock music provided an alternative, without falling into the pessimism of Allen Ginsberg's *Howl*. But there is more. Something in rock, with all its diverse forms, has caused modern society to assign it a major place in the cultural landscape.

Various Christian reactions

Dealing with 'the world' is forever the Church's challenge. When the Christian community offers answers in reaction to some current in the 'city of man', its deepest commitments are called into question. Its fears, its intelligence, its paradigms are unveiled as well. Opinions about rock music are no exception.

For some, anything goes, or almost. The Corinthian slogan 'all things are lawful', even with the Pauline corrective, encourages freedom in musical taste. Evil is in the eye of the beholder, apparently (I Cor. 6.2; 10.23), and so cultural forms are at worst neutral, at best good in themselves. Christian rock, even hard rock, is permissible and exploitable.

For others, rock is too trivial to bother. From Chuck Berry's silly high school proverbs to the modern lyrics of Prince, 'Dearly beloved we're gathered here today to get through this thing called life,' there seems little to be concerned about, if not the undue prolonging of adolescence.

Then for a third group, rock 'n' roll is essentially destructive and dangerous. The musical genre was developed to help alienate youth. Rock language, dress, and dance steps widen the gap. Stars are negative heroes, who lead abominable lives and delve into violence and sexual perversion. Conspiracy, political or occult, may be involved. David A. Noebel crusades against 'Rhythm, Riots and Revolution', finding evidence of Communist infiltration in a great deal of rock.[1] Conspiracy can work both ways. Recently a new lavender booklet called *How to Distinguish Decadent Songs* appeared in China.

What is the right attitude? What does the Bible say, if anything,

to guide us in this area? Is the answer simple? For experts only?
For kids only? Allow me to propose a classic approach. First, we
shall consider two extremes, both of which are to be avoided. Then
a third answer, or rather a 'third way', will be advanced.

The Manichean response

The first view I shall call Manichean. Manichaeism was a cult that
flourished from the third to the fifth century A.D. Its founder, Mani,
or Manes (216–c.277 AD), believed himself to be called at a very
young age to leave his Christian community and proclaim a new
doctrine which had been revealed to him. Some of his thinking is
quite involved, but the basic idea is easily grasped. Mani taught
radical dualism. Two principles exist in the universe, one of good
and the other of evil. The present world represents a mixture of the
two, and man himself has a dualistic nature. He is partly noble,
consubstantial with God, and partly base, having affinity with
matter. Until he can be set free to live in pure goodness, he is
'trapped' within a materialistic prison. Salvation, then, is obtained
through a kind of gnosis, a spiritual discernment which allows a
person to recognize the presence of matter and be released into
goodness.
    The danger of this view is its denial of the goodness of the created
world. Genesis 1.31 tells us that when God had finished the work
of creation, 'God saw all that he had made, and it was very good.'
While it is true that the world is now fallen because of man's
disobedience, the created world remains essentially good (Ps.
104.24, 28; 139.14). Matter has never been evil in the biblical view.
In Manichaeism, not only is the material world evil, but it lacks
substance. But Scripture tells us, 'Yea, the world is established, it
shall never be moved' (Ps. 96.10). While it is true that we wait for
heaven, which is a better place, there is continuity between the
world we know now and the world to come. Heaven is the world
made over, the creation set free (Rom. 8.21). The dualism of matter
and spirit, and the special gift of discernment needed to sort them
out, are notions entirely foreign to true Christiantiy.
    There is a widespread Manichean view of music. It translates to

the notion that certain purely musical elements are evil and can exercise a seductive power over the listener, manipulating or violating his being. A certain rhythm, for example, will tend to weaken a person's resistance to the baser side of life. Rock 'n' roll is a prime target for this view, although there exist many variations on it. One of the most outspoken and radical is set forth in a book with a video cassette, which is going around French-speaking countries, with the title (translated): *Rock 'n' Roll: Rape of the Conscience by Subliminal Messages*.[2] After a very cursory overview of the history of rock, the author tells of deliberate subversive signals, messages recorded backwards, speaking to the subconscious mind. Using a beat which accentuates the pulse, and hence sexual desires, coupled with high-pitched sounds which release extra endorphine into the body, rock music can force the subject to buy into its perverse message. He plays examples of rock songs read in reverse. Played backwards, the fuzzy sounds of Led Zeppelin's famous *Stairway to Heaven* seem to say, 'I've got to live for Satan'.

These opponents of rock are invariably concerned with immoral behaviour, drugs, insolent religious views, and Communist conspiracy. Some have a greater pastoral concern for the young people who are caught up in the rock seduction, which is commendable. But their methods are Manichean all the same. American evangelist Bob Larson's books often contain a glossary of rock groups in which he lists outrageous statements and scandalous behaviour found in their musicians. A similar approach leads John Blanchard to conclude that rock can *never* be used by Christians, either for evangelism or entertainment.[3]

Three serious problems with this approach hinder its effectiveness. The first is the tendancy toward extrapolation. So many of rock's opponents set forth a number of shocking examples, and then tell us all rock, and sometimes even blues or jazz, are necessarily committed to such decadence. Certainly there are repulsive rock groups. Who can stomach the blood-spitting, lascivious performances of Gene Simmons from Kiss, or the satanic lyrics of a song like *Sympathy for the Devil* by the Rolling Stones? Who is not shocked at some of the recent pornographic rock? Songs like *Treat Her Like a Prostitute* by the Get Fresh Crew go way beyond humour into cynical sexism. The lyrics are unprintable. Several groups have indulged in the occult, or in various forms of horror and violence. On their recent European tour, the Cramps performed their 'voodoo psychobilly', parading their obsessions with blood and evil.

And yet it is a serious mistake to lump all rock groups together and to reduce rock 'n' roll music to its darker side. The 'rock garden' is very diverse. The short quotes, impressions, and random statements picked up by rock's critics are not enough to justify such a sweeping view.

Many, if not most, rock musicians are just that. Musicians trying to succeed. Poring over the pages of *Rolling Stone, Melody Maker* and other magazines confirms this view. The interviewed musicians discuss their instruments, their tours, their songs, their problems with promoters, and so on. Most musicians in other branches can identify with the struggles and realities of performing rock groups. For all their notoriety, what the Rolling Stones enjoy doing most is playing the blues.[4]

While occasionally statements made by musicians represent a well thought out world view, more often there is something less momentous going on. Remarks in fact have different tones, light, sarcastic, ironic, or just plain silly. That in itself is perhaps significant. Messengers of a new ideal sometimes do use humour and in-talk to express their bonds with others in the movement. But more often in the case of rock musicians, the enigmatic humour is either for protection against an aggressive journalism, or even the awkwardness of youth. There is an openness, a kind of search for aesthetic principles expressed as well, which merely betrays the difference between a popular movement and a highly educated high-brow assurance.

One could seriously wonder whether there is any single force at all to rock over the last thirty years. After all, it is now the property of anyone under 50 years old. So many changes have occurred. We have rock for each ethnic group, for various age groups, for musical interest groups (hard rock, folk, funk, nostalgia). It is true that rock at the beginning seemed more unified than now. It had a certain spearhead. But even then, it is difficult to speak of it as a force which sought to have an impact. The early stars like Presley, Chuck Berry, Little Richard, and Buddy Holly were noticed by the media. The 1960s musicians like the Beatles, the Rolling Stones, and Bob

Dylan were media events. New technological means allowed rock to expand its range. Yet it is hard to imagine any kind of serious conspiracy here.

Certainly there are left-wing musicians who have social programmes inspired by hard-core socialism. Marxist sympathizers like Scritti Politti and the Redskins even try to use certain songs as a vehicle for their views. But an overall conspiracy such as that described by David Noebel is out of the question. In fact, rock 'n' roll had had a hard time of it in the Soviet Union! Russian Punk and New Wave groups like Zoo, Primus and Bravo, very popular with the young, have been thoroughly censored by the official organs and subjected to ideological control which has made performance almost impossible.[5]

As to real occult commitments, there are undoubtedly a number of rock stars seriously involved. But how widespread is it? Even the way-out Black Sabbath group does not seem really to believe in the existence of actual Satanic power. They use the trappings in jest, as publicity devices, but it is hard to affirm a hard-core commitment to the Devil. Of course, we must not be naive and think that such dabblings are harmless. My plea is for honesty in research methods. And I am also very concerned that the many musicians whose styles of life are whole and right should not be slandered merely by association. This dualism is unfair to the many excellent rock musicians.

The second major problem with the Manichean approach is the view that rock music manipulates the listener. By manipulation is meant controlling someone by unfair, insidious means. In this view, rock music contains a power which can corrupt youth and overcome the self-control of listeners by means of certain musical devices artfully employed.

This is a very ancient view, and one which is not simple to refute. Plato warned that listening to certain kinds of music would make citizens of his republic 'effeminate'.[6] In a number of countries, Protestants went so far as to forbid organ music in church, because of its mollifying effects on the worshippers. Recently music therapists have thought to turn this property to advantage, using the power of music to heal the distressed.

Are things so clear? Rock opponents like to cite behavioural psychologists who affirm the capacity to music to influence judgment and modify conduct. I have followed through with a number of these references, and have found that matters are not so clear cut. In point of fact, the state of modern research in this area is one of flux. An increasing body of material shows indeed that there is a correlation between music and physiological activities, such as respiration, cardiovascular patterns, and galvanic skin response. But even with these many variables enter in such as emotional predisposition, tiredness, educational level, musical ability, making prediction very difficult.[7] This is not even to mention moral response, where experiments show no consistent patterns at all. Nor have experiments revealed any measurable effects from the backward-masking process.

The same goes for the relation of the occult to music. In a remarkable 500–page work, ethnomusicologist Gilbert Rouget reports on a nearly exhaustive study of the correlation between music and the state of trance.[8] His balanced and scientific approach led him to compare hundreds of situations where people were brought into a state of trance, where music is present as well. He did observe the frequent and important connection between musical events and the trance. But what could not be established was a predictable pattern. Music may be present or absent for the trance to take place. When it is present, no one style, no particular set of instruments, no required decibel-level, no rhythmic type are necessarily used. While music is there as a social factor, nothing in the *musical substance* can be shown to condition possession or trance.[9]

The grain of truth contained in the Manichean idea of manipulation is that music is a symbol system. It does articulate meaning. As a cultural phenomenon it has the capacity to communicate. We will want to say more about this later. But for the present, what needs to be emphasized is that rock music indeed has a message. But it does not put it across primarily by subliminal manipulation. It does so the way all cultural forms do, by its own architecture, by the images and words which accompany the sounds.

Again, I want to stress that there are rock groups that practise sorcery, load the dice with *double entendre*, backward-masking, and so on. But we have no proof that there can be any effect against the will of the listener. In some ways, the direct attack may have more impact. When the Sex Pistols announce in one of their songs, 'I am the antichrist, I am an anarchist, don't know what I want, but I know how to get it', we are in the presence of something dreadful. But can it force us against our wills into a primal rebellion? This brings us to the third major problem.

The real power of music

In the Manichean view it is a particular accoustical property of rock which can corrupt the listener: the rhythmic pulse, the high volume, the fuzz-tone of the amplifier, etc. For this reason, not only does it have a fascination which draws one into its web, but simply being in attendance when the music is played puts one's morals into jeopardy.

The difficulty here is that while there may be manifestations of evil in cultural forms, evil itself is not a thing. It is a revolt, a state of rebellion, a *contra boni*. There are results in every area of life, which includes art and music. But these results take on different aspects according to the particular part of reality which evil affects. A disease or a wound is a result which is physical. In theological terms, we would say disease is a consequence of the Fall. The human suffering produced by the disease is a painful reaction which is, of course, negative. A sick human being may be tempted to fall into rebellion against God because of the presence of that negative factor. But neither the disease nor the suffering are themselves capable of provoking the evil of rebellion.

Music as a cultural form may express or articulate good or evil. At least it may do so in musical terms. The specific ways in which music 'speaks' are not always easy to describe. Correlations between musical shapes and audience reaction are not always clear either. (When lyrics accompany the music things may be more clear, although the words to a song are more than just a 'key' to its meaning.) However, as Christians it is crucial to assert that no physical or cultural thing can force one to compromise morals. Only deliberate choice can do that.

There is a remarkable passage in Saint Augustine's *Confessions* which describes an episode in the life of Alypius, one of the author's friends and disciples.[10] It sheds much light on the present concern. After hearing his master lecture on Proverbs 9.8, the young Alypius was convicted of sin, and felt himself particularly rebuked for his worldly love of the gladiatorial games. He decided never to go again. In Rome, as a student, however, his fellow students bullied and badgered him, until he finally let himself to dragged to the arena for a game. 'You may drag me there bodily', he protested, 'but do you imagine that you can make me watch the show and give my mind to it? I shall be there, but it will be just as if I were not present, and I shall prove myself stronger than you or the games!' Such was his confident boast.

Unfortunately, although Alypius closed his eyes, he didn't close his ears. At one point the crowd roared, and 'this thrilled him so deeply that he could not contain his curiousity'. He opened his eyes, confident that he would be repulsed rather than giving in. But then he fell into the excitement and let himself go. 'He revelled in the wickedness of the fighting and was drunk with the fascination of bloodshed.' In the end, he even became a leader, dragging others to the arena as he had been dragged.

Now this story is almost embarrassing for me, because it comes so close to disproving my point! But wait. Augustine's final remark is this: 'Yet you stretched out your almighty, ever merciful hand, O God, and rescued him from this madness. You taught him to trust in you, not in himself. But this was much later.' A terrible and deadly struggle is represented here, between three powerful forces. The enemy is the bloodlust and decadence of the ancient world. Against it is pitted the force of self-control, inner determination, the enlightened morality of this same classical culture. Stoic, Epicurian and Manichean ethics are the *summum* of that age. Yet they cannot withstand the onslaught; they are swept away by the power of the mass, by sense manipulation. Augustine's friend is crushed; but along with him the rationalistic philosophy of the ancient world is also defeated. A third force emerges. It is Christianity, with its wholly different approach to ethics.[11] Self-control is not enough. Only trusting God's will can help, a trust that provides strength against the chaotic forces of evil, giving a strength far deeper and far more hopeful than Greek philosophy.

Saint Augustine is teaching us that with the Lord we can indeed resist, but we go far beyond mere resistance. God's strength is not only more powerful, but able to save, able to redeem. It can do this because it recognizes the true nature of the enemy. The Manicheans, whom Augustine knew well, were incapable of such a recognition because they identified evil as a thing or a substance. But real evil is the mysterious desire for autonomy. The root seduction of them all is idolatry.

The arena indeed! There are parallels between many rock concerts and the games. But Stoic resistance to musical substance misses the point. The point is the evil of idolatry and the power of God to redeem the world, even the world of music. Have you ever carefully watched the video-clips on television which bombard the screens? They often set forth a counterfeit religion, carrying all the elements of neopaganistic ritual. The cut-up scenes and absurd sequences confuse and baffle our sense of sequence, preparing us for something less rational. The mysterious, smokey atmosphere, the steady, dull pulse, set the scene for the modern high priests, carrying their electronic ceremonial gear, sacrificing on the altar of hedonism. Here is idolatry far more subtle than subliminal messages.

The relativist response

The second view which we want to consider is one that basically says music is neutral. Its only impact is because of social or psychological association. Perhaps you have the impression from my argument against the Manichean view that I would hold to the relativist response myself. While I do think that there are many social and psychological factors which are involved in our reaction to a given piece of music, I do not think that music is neutral.

A Christian version of the relativist response claims the New Testament teaching on the religious implications of eating food. 'No food is unclean in itself. But if anyone regards something as unclean, then for him it is unclean', says the Apostle Paul (Rom. 14.14). But matters are not so simple. It is clear from the context here that Paul is not declaring every part of the world pure and good. His point is that food is no longer ceremonially considered, in the new age.

That is, under the Old Covenant, certain foods were declared off bounds for pedagogical reasons. It was a way of remembering the uniqueness of being a Jew. This had nothing to do with the quality of the food, nor was it connected with hygiene. It was a ceremonial practice which was done away with in Christ. In Romans 14 Paul draws attention to the error of those who continue to respect the ceremonial law about foods. But he also cautions the more mature believers against parading their liberty in regards to food in front of other brothers who have not quite arrived at that state of maturity; that is, those who are still concerned to respect such distinctions, because their conscience is tender. For those who are less free, then, food is still unclean in a sense. Their feelings about it lead them to that conclusion. But in fact it isn't so, because food was created by God and therefore good in itself.

We do not imagine Paul saying, for example, murder is clean in itself, but unclean for those who think so. The difference between food and social ethics is clear. Food in itself is good. There is, of course, bad food (rotten, poisonous, etc.). But here Paul is talking about normal, well-prepared food. The reason it is good is, as he reminds another set of his readers in a similar vein, that 'The earth is the Lord's, and everything in it' (I Cor. 10.26).

Eating food is a cultural practice, as well as a natural necessity. This makes Paul's discussions about food particularly relevant to our considerations about music. The Apostle does not lift food out of its cultural context, saying in effect, 'smart Christians realize that food is good and that all of these cultural conventions surrounding it are merely relative'. His point is much subtler. To the Corinthian Church Paul argued similarly as he had to the Romans (see I Cor. 8.4–13; 10.14–31). But the problem is a bit different in this case. What should Christians do about meat offered to idols? His answer is twofold. First, idols are nothing, and so the food offered to them is not contaminated thereby (8.4–6; 10.19, 25–27). Second, however, do not participate in the ceremony which marks the connection between sacrificed foods and the demons behind the idols, which are real. This is partly for the sake of others watching you (8.7–13; 10.23–24; 28–30), and partly because God forbids the practices associated with demon worship (8.10; 10.14–18, 20–22).

So food is not neutral. It is either good because created by God and received with thanksgiving (I Cor. 10.31, I Tim. 4.1 ff.), or bad because offered to demons. In the latter case, the reason to abstain is not because of biological corruption in the food, but because the meaning of the food is transformed into part of a forbidden ethical practice.

The parallels with music can be made, if very cautiously. We might notice at the outset that music has a much greater capacity to articulate meaning than food-eating practices. Also, music is a human practice, less directly related to God's created world than food. Yet the analogy still holds. One could say the ability to make music is God-given. Jubal, the father of instrumental music, produced meaningful sounds because God made man to produce cultural artifacts (Gen. 1.28–30; 4.21). Using Rouget's terminology, we might say, God enabled man to produce musical substance: pitch, rhythm, timbre, and so on. However, the next step is to say that the way men and women put these sounds together carries a meaning. In an unfallen world, this meaning would have been good, just as all food-eating practices would have been good. But in a fallen world, music can articulate error as well as truth; as it did in fact right from the earliest times in the boastful song of Jubal's father Lamech (Gen. 4.23–24).

If Paul could say, 'an idol is nothing' (I Cor. 8.4; 10.19), he would not say 'an idol sculpted to articulate pagan meaning is a failure'. It is only 'nothing' in that the stone, the head, the legs, etc. do not carry a demonic charge, as it were, as a wire carries electric energy. Many idols, in fact, are wonderfully made and speak very eloquently of pagan realities. They can even be admired from an artistic viewpoint and collected by museums. But when one respects the cultural context, there is no neutrality in the idol.

For music, it is the same. Music articulates a certain meaning, because it is a human, cultural activity. This does not mean that music is a discourse on ideologies, world views, and so on. The way music means is particular to music. In fact, there is no one category for meaning. We can discuss the meaning of life, or the meaning of a green light, or the meaning of a poem. None of these is exactly the same discussion. So then we must decide what we are looking for when we discuss musical meaning. Are we concerned to discover a verbal message behind the music? Can a piece of music tell us it's a beautiful day, or that unemployment is up, or that Mary is happy? Putting the matter this way gives us a clue to the meaning of music. While occasionally composers try to portray scenes or emotions through musical conventions (programme music does this), surely they can never limit musical meaning merely to some verbal or psychological equivalent. Music must *mean* in its own way, through its particular structures.

This is not to imply that there are no norms which can be described verbally. Words are indispensable in order to arrive at the sense of sounds. But they must respect the rich ways in which music carries that sense. An analogy from the world of painting may help. We could compare the meaning of two paintings using the same motif. Both Rembrandt and Francis Bacon painted a side of beef. The comparison is revealing. While both paintings are highly competent, the feeling is very different. Rembrandt's side of beef exhibits a coherent whole. The colours, the composition tell us that this object fits into an orderly world. Rembrandt is fascinated by the object because it allows him to explore the folds, the lines, the intriguing shapes of this totally ordinary thing. It challenges his craft. Bacon's painting carries a very different meaning. One sees only an absurd ensemble of intestines, blood, horror. It is 'more' than a side of beef, it is a symbol of the torn, irrational world which the painter believes to be the real one. All of this is achieved through painting conventions, not words.

To artistic conventions, social and cultural ones may be added, not as a compromise with a purely artistic expression, but because nothing exists in a vacuum. Social conventions do not detract from music's meaning since music, like the other art forms, is partly a social product. Thus, the 'meaning of meaning' for the arts in general, and for music in particular, includes many dimensions. The sense of a musical compostion is not merely its *substance*, but the complex of the components which make it up, and which can be described verbally as well as felt subjectively. The orchestral work *La Mer*, by Claude Debussy, carries its meaning in the rhythms, tonalities, timbres, and the structure of the piece. The effect of the compositions depends on the listener's cultural background as well. This particular work builds on the succession of small units, musical mobiles which appear and disappear in sequence. The very difference between this construction and the classical sonata form, with its theme introduced, developed and recapitulated, is crucial to the way it means. With a hundred devices at his disposal, Debussy achieves various levels of meaning, including the mysterious portrayal of a world outside of our own for which he was well known.

Some would argue that the appreciation of music is primarily a question of taste. Perhaps so, but taste is not a simple notion. Certainly taste is involved when preferring rugby to football or peaches to pears. But surely in this case, we are talking about the diversity of life's offerings, which is extremely important, and yet not to be confused with the question of standards. Taste can also be related to objective factors. We speak about educating taste, acquiring taste, improving taste, precisely because more is involved than subjective factors. In music, as well, taste sometimes involves just the diversity of styles and the personal preferences for one over the other. But at other times we are dealing with the aesthetics of the piece, the virtues of a composition.

Pure aesthetic relativism is not only impossible but undesirable. If we are God's image-bearers, neutral activities are not feasible. Admittedly activities such as music-making are especially hard to evaluate. The hardship of relegating the arts to neutrality is even less desirable.

The Manichean approach has grasped something of this aspect of rock music, but its methods and attitudes have led it off the track. The dualist presupposition of the analysis hinders it from seeing the real meaning structure involved. But relativism does the same thing in the end, since it acknowledges no norms at all, or only very limited ones. There is not much bargain between the two!

The message of rock

After all of these preliminaries and qualifiers you may well be asking: well all right, what *is* the meaning of rock? Let us look at a number of aspects of the question.

The various kinds of rock 'n' roll music carry a musical meaning particular to the genre. Rock is popular music. As such, it has ties with folk music with its aptitude for communicating the shared feelings of a human society. As we have said, it has a heavy debt of rhythm and blues, a derivation of the older black American styles, which also have a particular meaning structure. The 'blue note', for example, which is achieved by bending the third, fifth, or seventh of a diatonic scale, communicates the down-to-earth realism and at the same time the spiritual longing that characterized the aspirations of the black American community. Also, there is a certain optimism in the blues which is is partly carried in its A-A-B structure, a kind of question and answer form which resembles the poetic pattern of the Old Testament wisdom literature. In rock, these elements are generally simplified or exaggerated, which has sometimes led to an impoverishment of the genre. Occasionally, the commercial side of rock has obscured this more authentic derivation, so that high decibels, the glitter of entertainers, needless repetition have intruded. But the roots are there.

This I believe is what makes rock able to articulate a certain realism which much sentimental show music cannot. To qualify as rock, there must be some element of challenge, even rebellion. Many rock musicians are aware of this demension, although not all of them realize the importance of it. Wendy Melvoin and Lisa Coleman, who currently accompany superstar Prince, recently commented on this aspect of rock 'n' roll. Their problem is that their own parents were 'total beatniks, then hippies'. Lisa adds, 'they used to joke that to rebel we'd have to turn into staunch Republicans, but we just took their lives and went one step further'.[12] Taking things one step further is not necessarily a clear manifesto. But it does imply a calling into question of modern life. That is essential to rock. Allow me to quote at some length from a recent story in *Melody Maker*. It is an article on the Three Johns, a popular English group:

Explain rock 'n' roll against Thatcherism.
   'It's self-explanatory, isn't it?' says John Brennan. 'Rock 'n' roll, by definition, is against Thatcherism. And if it *isn't*, it's not rock 'n' roll.'
   It's not the contention so much as its self-explanatory nature that irks. This common ground of consensus that invariably

allows interviews to move quickly to the important business – the
Red Stripe, the jibes and snipes at Reagan and Thatcher – without
pausing to consider who's listening, what the extent of the threat
is.

And this assumption that there's a natural fit between rock and
socialism . . . Isn't rock's energy intensely individualistic, selfish,
even anti-social? Aren't there energies and drives in rock that
oppose any form of social organization?

John Hiatt sees no conflict. 'Rock 'n' roll is the expression of
the individual in a hostile environment. Hopefully real socialism
would be for the better expression of the individual *within* a
collective society.'

Brennan continues: 'I'd say rock 'n' roll should always be anti-
establishment – whatever the establishment is.'[13]

Admittedly the element of rebellion is not always perceived as such
by the musicians. Furthermore, the 'expression of the individual in
a hostile environment' is not always directed toward positive
solutions. In a word, rock rebellion is often arbitrary. There are
often mixed motives as well. This is why the idea of a conspiracy
is so short-sighted. Of course, there is no single force behind rock 'n'
roll, a sort of general consensus pushing for change of orientation. At
the same time, there is very often a search for a kind of authenticity
which materialism does not offer.

This is why some rock is pornographic, some is violent, while
some is more 'spiritual'. A great deal of rock in the 1960s and '70s
was socially conscious. Reggae music originated in Jamaica out of
concern for the unemployed masses. Punk rock answered back,
from Bromley in South East London, that there were no answers.
Anarchistic, the mechanical beat of groups like Ultraviolet lashes
out against 'the establishment', even against religion (as they do
in their popular album *New Testament*), but without giving any
alternatives. Yet many groups continue to express social concern
and seem to long after political peace and justice.

In many ways, hard rock is closest to black American roots,
because the music is so akin to the urban blues of the 1940s, albeit
modified with impressive electronic means. So, although musicians
like Ozzy Osbourne from this genre are attracted to the occult

and to violence, there is something real and down-to-earth in their rebellion.

The softer sounds of folk rock are perhaps the most appropriate to responsible social criticism. And the commercial sounds of the 'Top 40' hit parade are perhaps the farthest from this awareness. But the trait of a search for authenticity is still an essential ingredient in all of rock 'n' roll, though by no means the only one. In a way, this should not surprise us. If music carries cultural meaning, it should reflect certain trends in modern life. David Lyon has shown, masterfully, that we are in a secularized world, and that the essence of secularization is the search for boundaries.[14] The Church no longer supplies a moral framework or legitimation, and yet so far nothing has taken its place in order to do so. Rock music has an important part in carrying this meaning:

> The most prominent vehicle for the transmission of 'liminoid' (boundary-questioning) culture is rock music and, more gener- ally, what is usually referred to as 'youth culture'. Not thought and calculation, but play and experience are the outstanding quali- ties of 'rock'. Not cerebral but celebratory. The messages of rock music are overwhelmingly hedonistic – but nevertheless carry their own 'orderliness' with them.[15]

This is an important statement. Of course, there is a good deal of narcissism in rock culture. But it still qualifies as a kind of search for authenticity.

This is why many have noticed the 'salvation' message of 'the rock experience'. There is something in the music which enables it to offer a unique invitation. If you listen to rock, you can 'have it both ways', you can be political and beyond politics, down-to-earth and yet on a 'trip', in tune, and yet 'turned-on'.[16] To consider but one example, the music of Prince is pregnant with this kind of meaning. His recent album *Music From Under the Cherry Moon* (Paisley Park, Warner Brothers) testifies to his penchant for the mystique of rock. The libido is fully exploited in a message of redemption through feeling. Rooted in black American tradition, the songs are nevertheless inspired by his own search for authen- ticity. Of course, as was the case in his film *Purple Rain*, it is the music that saves. The secularity of the world is felt in these sub-

Christian, at times idolatrous songs. Still, the search is there, and it is sincere.

Christian counterpoint

In closing, I'd like to make three suggestions. They are not meant to be formulas for success, but rather proposals for tasks that Christians may take on in order to be able to deal with some of the larger questions that have been raised here.

First, I believe we need to elaborate a proper language of popular music aesthetics. Many books and articles on rock attempt, with more or less success, to evaluate this powerful phenomenon. In the process terms are used, and a certain language for speaking about the music in relation to meaning evolves. But we often find that categories are used which have no biblical basis, and thus the language is limited or even inappropriate. John Blanchard, for example, tells us there is no such thing as Christian music and non-Christian music. There is only good and bad music. From these categories a certain vocabulary, a certain language is implied. Very well, but what is good music? How do we best describe it? Does Scripture give us a list of qualities to look for? Upon examination, we find that there is no 'eleventh commandment' on obedient art. But then we begin to realize the Bible does not speak this way about many other things, such as marriage, agriculture, education; yet it has much to say in all these areas. There is little detail, for example, on how to recognize a beautiful face, yet such loveliness is often spoken of. There are no verses telling me how often a day I must speak to my wife, or how to hold down a carpentry tool. The Bible doesn't speak in a succession of dictionary definitions because it is not a dictionary. Also, there is harmony between God's creation, with its 'general revelation', and the covenantal words of his special revelation. Subduing the earth (Gen. 1.28) is a matter of understanding this harmony, and of developing the linguistic tools necessary to this God-given task.

Describing rock 'n' roll is no different from describing marriage. Where does this music fit in as covenant activity in the aspect of sound? What kind of blues guitar is really skilful? What are the boundaries for a popular music that promotes sounds and rhythms that do well on the market? What is a sane and biblically-wise use of electronic equipment? How can this music be an appropriate vehicle to communicate truth in all its aspects, without falling into propaganda? Our proper language of popular music aesthetics will have to deal with all these. The language will need to be developed by musicians, theologians, believers, critics and others, before we can responsibly decide on certain aspects of rock music.

Second, we need to elaborate what we might call the principle of redemption, as we deal with rock music. By using this term, I don't want for one minute to take away from the once-for-all totally sufficient work of our Lord. I want instead to describe our secondary responsibility as heirs of his grace here on earth. Because we live *in* the world, yet without being *of* the world (John 17.14–16), we constantly need to *filter* things in the light of biblical norms. There is a Pauline principle which helps us here: 'Test everything. Hold on to the good' (I Thess. 5.21). Notice that it is basically positive: keep the good parts, prune off the bad. So often we do the reverse: hold up the bad and avoid it, and leave off worrying about the good. In the Bible 'testing' (or 'proving') means to evaluate, and much more. It has to do with the way we try things out to know if they are good. It encourages us to have contact with things around us in order to decide what to do with them. The word is used in the parable of the wedding feast: 'I have bought five yoke of oxen, and I'm on my way *to try them out*, please excuse me' (Luke 14.19). It is also used in I Timothy about deacons in the Church. First they should be proved, before ordaining them (I Tim. 3.10).

Because the world is a mixed place of good and evil, not in the Manichean sense but because of creation, fall and redemption, our purpose should be to try things out and see if there is a good to be held to. What rock may we listen to? What groups use techniques helpful for our purposes? Rather than establish an evangelical index, my plea is to go ahead and explore this varied world of rock 'n' roll: the dance-oriented music of the black groups, Dylan's prophetic folk rock, the mechanical beat of Punk, and New Wave, even the blander sounds of background music. Why not? Isn't some piped-in music a help in daily living? If all of these rockish sounds are part of the sound track, let's prove them and see what can be done to redeem them and 'sing a new song unto the Lord'. At the moment, is the best we can do Live Aid, with 'We are the World', an amalgam of singers and ideas based on a common denominator? Can we do better? It seems so often that Christian rock groups are caught in a dilemma. Either they white-wash the form and surgically remove its power, or they so totally identify with it that we wonder whether there is any redeeming presence at all. Yet if the search for authenticity is of the essence in rock, may we not use it for our own purposes?

Proving can be very radical. It must go beyond just testing-to-be-sure-nothing-is-wrong! Recently the Christian 'heavy metal' band Stryper, one of the few to have success on the secular pop charts, explained their approach. Dressed in full regalia, with complement of fabulous amplifying equipment, they seek to evangelize, to 'win their listeners' hearts after capturing their attention'. The music is thus a kind of prelude, and is as heavy-metal as possible. Their reasoning: 'You don't have to compromise on the music or the look as long as sin doesn't mix in with it!'[17] That gives me problems. Reduced to its barest forms, the argument says we can be like the world until the red light goes on. But the approach of 'as-worldly-as-possible' misses the point of proving, which is *im*proving. Musicians like James Ward, the group U2, and others are doing this today.

Third, and last, let us be sure to consider the social background of rock. Although I disagree strongly with the Manichean view, I do appreciate the pastoral concern of some of its exponents. Bob Larson looks for family problems like communication gaps behind surface tensions over the young person's love for rock. There often is one. Parents can't be bothered, or won't take time to listen. Young people don't see the sense of sharing their private world of musical taste. Rock, after all, was meant to widen the generation gap. But one of the best ways for Christian families to handle the delicate problem of listening habits is to sit down together, go over a few records carefully, discuss the strengths and weaknesses in an atmosphere free of resentment. I have tried this with our own children, and what an education it has been for me! It has helped me discover musicians I had not known about. It has also helped my children to feel we are in this proving business all together. And it can work the other way, too. I haven't 'converted' our own children to Duke Ellington yet, but I am trying, and have hopes! As was said earlier, there is nothing wrong with modifying taste, provided it is for the right reasons. This may prove the hardest obstacle of all, not just for young people but for adults as well. The above-mentioned view that rock is not worth bothering about is the approach of the Christian ostrich.

For some reason, church people do not like being challenged in the area of art. Calvin Seerveld puts it wonderfully:

> If a medical doctor tells a person to cut the fat out of his diet or he'll have a heart attack, one does it and starts eating Rye Krisp and a lot of cottage cheese. If a doctor of aesthetics tells a person to sell all his chrome and plastic kitchen furniture and have a garage sale on the overstuffed living room sofa or risk a life of materialistic superficiality, one would tell such a doctor to mind his own business. Why?[18]

Why indeed? Because we are too used to relegating art to amusement or luxury. We don't realize that art is a cultural calling, with its own area of sovereignty. Art is a way of seeing, as well as creation; it is a vehicle for understanding the world, as well as enjoying it. It may be ambiguous, delightfully so, because its nature is to be rich in imagery, symbol and representation. This is what makes propaganda art boring, incidentally, because it has left the sphere of the heuristic. Here we have a clue to at least one of the norms of art we will want to identify. Music as art, then, has its own structures and ways of meaning. Rock 'n' roll is a particular kind of music, born in our times, a special modern style-language. But it has rules and norms and can be improved. Like a foreign language, it will have to be learned before it can be evaluated. Even our taste must be educated! Such education will be nourished on historical, social, and cultural considerations; for nothing, especially in art, exists in a vacuum. The ultimate norm will be the word of God, which itself was elaborated in the context of redemptive history.

These proposals may seem impossible, humanly. There is so much work to do. We have fallen dreadfully behind. And culture is one of those things that cannot be rushed. However, let me say reverently, God is in no human hurry. Remember Martin Luther's remark, when a monk asked him what he would do if he knew the Lord was returning that day: I would plant a tree, he said. In this perspective, nothing is impossible, even the redemption of rock culture!

Notes

1. David A. Noebel, *Rhythm, Riots and Revolution*, Tulsa, Okla., 1966.
2. Jean-Paul Regimbal et al., *Le rock 'n' roll* [sic.], *viol de la conscience par les messages subliminaux*, Geneva, 1983.
3. John Blanchard, *Pop Goes the Gospel*, Welwyn, 1983, pp.75–90, 111–17.
4. Jonathan Cott and Sue Clark; 'Mick Jagger', in *The Rolling Stone Interviews*, vol. 1, New York, 1971, p.162.
5. Terry Bright, 'Soviet Crusade Against Pop', in *Popular Music*, vol. 5, Cambridge, 1985, pp.141 ff.
6. Plato, *The Republic*. Book III.
7. See, for example, G. and H. Harrer, 'Music, Emotion and Automatic Function', in M. Critcheley and R. A. Henson, eds., *Music and the Brain*, London, 1977, pp.202–16. See also Parliamentary Assembly of the Council of Europe, 37th Ordinary Session, 'Sound and Private Life,' Strasbourg, 1985.
8. Gilbert Rouget, *La Musique et la Transe*, Paris, 1980.
9. Ibid. pp.438–42. The growing field of music therapy uses sound for the well-being for a subject. Therapists believe strongly in the power of music, but in most works I have consulted, the connections are not made clear, and the case remains for Rouget's view. Nothing in the actual musical substance operates on the individual. Other factors are always present.
10. Augustine, *The Confessions*, VI.8.
11. See the brilliant analysis of this passage by Erich Auerbach, *Mimesis*, Garden City, NY, 1957, pp.59–66.

12. Neal Karlen, 'Wendy Lisa and Prince: A Musical Love Affair', in *Rolling Stone*, No. 472, April 24, 1986, p.46.

13. Alan Reevell, 'Social Surrealists', in *Melody Maker*, May 17, 1986, p.14.

14. See David Lyon, *The Steeple's Shadow*, London, 1985, pp.140ff.

15. Ibid., p.109.

16. Benjamin DeMott, 'Rock Saves?', in *Supergrow: Essays and Reports on Imagination in America*, New York, 1969, p.55.

17. *Christianity Today*, February 15, 1985, p.46.

18. Calvin Seerveld, *Rainbows for the Fallen World*, Toronto, 1980, p.45.

God and our Books

by Ruth Etchells

Many people hold the view, either in secret or in public, that the arts, and particularly literature, are a sheer waste of time when it comes to 'real life'. It is an attitude sometimes held by Christians who should know better, and I want to challenge it.

It is very important that we take reading seriously if we are Christians, called to be in the world at a particular time and in a particular place. Why? That is a huge question, and I want to consider it with you in three main areas.

Firstly, what are the trends of modern and even contemporary literature, that is, the literature which expresses our age, and has shaped and is shaping our consciousness?

Secondly, is the question of literary judgement (how do I judge what I read?) simply a matter of personal taste, or are there any objective criteria?

Thirdly, how can Christians develop a distinctively Christian approach to literature?

1. What are the trends of this century's literature?

Let me say at once, mine is a personal view. For everybody there is a different 'modern literature' – that is one of the problems of dealing with it. I am giving you a personal, 'Etchells', perspective. But one or two of its ingredients are, I think, arguable across the whole range of opinion.

Firstly, it can be argued that literature of this century is *intensely serious*. It is not frivolous at all. It takes life, and its speculations about life, with the utmost seriousness. And it is because of that, and not because of superficiality, that it is often scatological, that there is the sense of corruption and despair in so much that is written. One might, for example, compare it with the savagery of Dean Swift in *Gulliver's Travels* and other writings. It arises as it arose with him; much of the semi-pornography and intense anger and insult in language is coming from an intense realization of how serious things are.

It is the more serious because today's writers feel that upon them has been placed the diagnostic and prophetic role left vacant by the loss of confidence in the Church and in those who stand for the Church. Let me quote a moving passage from a contemporary and very great American writer, Nobel Prize winner Saul Bellow:

To understand . . . you have to think first of modern literature as a sort of grand council considering what mankind should do next, how we should fill our mortal time, what we should feel, where we should get our courage, how we should love or hate, how we should be pure or great or terrible, evil (you know!) and all the rest. This advice of literature has never done much good. But you see, God doesn't rule over men as he used to, and for a long time people haven't been able to feel that life was firmly attached at both ends so that they could confidently stand in the middle. That kind of faith is missing, and for many years poets have tried to supply a substitute. Like the 'unacknowledged legis-lators' or 'the best is yet to be' or Walt Whitman saying that whoever touched him could be sure he was touching a man. Some have stood up for beauty and some have stood up for perfect proportion, and the very best have soon gotten tired of art for its own sake. Some took it as their duty to behave like brave performers who try to hold down panic during a theatre fire. Very great ones have quit, like Tolstoy who becomes a reformer, or like Rimbaud, who went to Abyssinia, and as the end of his life was begging of a priest, 'Montrez-mois. Montrez . . . Show me something.' Frightening. Frightening . . . Maybe they assumed too much responsibility. They knew that if by their poems and novels *they* were fixing values, there must be something wrong with the values. No one man can furnish them. (From the short story, *Dr Mosby's Memoirs*.)

What is the focus of this seriousness? Looking over the literature
of the last fifty years, from the 1930s to the 1980s, two words sum
up for me the main foci: 'dereliction', and – unexpectedly – 'hope'.
They are the twin poles of today's serious writers. A poem of the
1960s expresses this quite clearly, in fairly facile imagery:

> I think they will remember this as the age of lamentations
> The age of broken minds and broken souls,
> The age of hurt creatures sobbing out their sorrow to the
>   rhythm of the blues –
> The music of lost Africa's desolation become the music
>   of the town.
> The age of failure of splendid things
> The age of the deformity of splendid things.
> The age of old young men and bitter children,
> The age of treachery and of a great new faith.
> The age of madness and machines,
> Of broken bodies and fear twisted hearts.
>
> The age of frenzied fumbling and possessive lusts –
> And yet, deep down, an age unsatisfied by dirt and guns,
> An age which though choken by the selfishness of the few who
>   owned their bodies and their souls,
> Still struggled blindly to the end,
> And in their time reached out magnificently
> Even for the very stars themselves.
>
>   (H.D. Carberry, 'Epitaph')

Under the popular imagery, there emerges very clearly the age's
sense of the grubbiness, sordidness, despair and sense of failure and
disappointment, set against that unquenchable vision, that 'going
onwards', which is seen even in our age as characteristic of man.
Both those themes appear, much more profoundly, in a wide range
of modern writing.

From Saul Bellow's heroes, all of whom are looking for that
which – against the frenetic seeking for satisfaction of the age – will
still the cry in their hearts of 'I want! I want! I want!'

On from Bellow to John Osborne, writing out of grief and anger
at what our age has done to the liveliness of the love lyric such as

Shakespeare and John Donne wrote: so that lines like 'Shall I compare thee to a summer's day? Thou art more lovely and more temperate' have been transmuted in our times into, amongst other things, a series of advertisements of hard porn in videos and blue books. Right across the range, what characterizes our age's sense of *dereliction* as it appears in contemporary writing, is of something *spoilt:* spoliation, desecration, disjunction, the disordering of harmony, the trampling of daffodils. Paradise is lost, even though there is no agreement about what constitutes Paradise anyway. The Paradise of Empire is transmuted into 'staying on'. The Paradise of Shelter, or Home and Security, is transmuted (in *The Caretaker*, for instance) into caretaking for someone else, and then being moved on. And this sense of the spoilt, the lost, shows itself in various obsessive themes: in, for instance, a morbid sensitivity about death, particularly its physical horror and quenching of vitality. Here is the penultimate paragraph of a great novel, Muriel Spark's *Memento Mori*, with its telephone message – 'Remember you must die' – repeated throughout the book to its end:

> What were they sick, what did they die of? Lettie Colston, he recited to himself, comminuted fractures of the skull; Godfrey Colston, hypostatic pneumonia; Charmian Colston, uraemia; Jean Taylor, myocardial degeneration; Tempest Sidebottome, carcinoma of the cervix; Ronald Sidebottome, carcinoma of the bronchus; Guy Leet, arteriosclerosis, Henry Mortimer, coronary thrombosis . . .

It is a litany of our age's terror and horror at the knowledge of death.

Put against that, Dylan Thomas's words:

> Do not go gentle into that good night,
> Old age should burn and rage at close of day;
> Rage, rage against the dying of the light . . .
> Good men, the last wave by, crying how bright
> Their frail deeds might have danced in a green bay,
> Rage, rage against the dying of the light . . .
> Do not go gentle into that good night.
> Rage, rage against the dying of the light.
>
> ('Do not go gentle into that good night')

The horror of death is upon us; nothing new, but very vivid: 'Timor mortis conturbat me'. There's a valuable book to be written about the handling of death in our modern literature.

Death can obviously be seen as the ultimate spoiling. But the grief and dereliction of life, in its loss of certainty and its individual pain, is the hymn of the age too. David Gascoyne, for instance, speaks about individual dereliction, of the total and abject distress to which one can be reduced:

> Here am I now cast down
> Beneath the black glare of a netherworld's
> Dead suns, dust in my mouth, among
> Dun tiers no tears refresh: am cast
> Down by a lofty hand.
>
> ('Miserere')

Perhaps even more profoundly despairing is the vision of a nihilistic universe; not just an individual contracted and broken, but the entire cosmos, a cosmos pointless, emptied of content, barren of significance, causeless and meaningless. Beckett, of course, portrays it in *Waiting for Godot*. Much more recently, Golding in *Darkness Visible*, describing what I think is our most contemporary sense of despair and horror, of a universe running down not mechanistically, but philosophically and spiritually. Our generation of the 1980s has very powerfully recovered the sense of the numinous. But what is terrifying is that it is numinous *evil* of which our generation is profoundly conscious, as much, if not more than, numinous good. Joseph Conrad's terrible vision of evil, dominating the vision of the universe in *The Heart of Darkness*, has found its echo in the 1980s, in Golding's vision of the power of evil that is disintegrative of the moral as well as the physical universe: 'entropy' – the falling to pieces of our inner and outer worlds. One of the characters in *Darkness Visible* who gives herself up totally to that experience and whatever powers there are that manipulate it, the dark powers, says:

Everything's running down. Unwinding. We're just – tangles. Everything is just a tangle and it slides out of itself bit by bit towards something that's simpler and simpler – and we are disappearing with it.

Very frightening!

That is powerfully reminiscent of some of Milton's darker visions in *Paradise Lost*. Oh yes, our literature is serious. And running in and out of all that lies our own sense of wrong and failure and guilt: from John Arden to Tom Stoppard, from Peter Shaffer to Margaret Drabble and Edna O'Brien, there is a sense of humanity spoiling itself, robbing itself, destroying itself.

Here, written some twenty years ago now, is John Wain's poem, 'The Bad Thing', which expresses it with exactitude:

> Sometimes just being alone seems the bad thing.
> Solitude can swell until it blocks the sun.
> It hurts so much, even fear, even worrying
> Over past and future, get stifled. It has won,
> You think; this is the bad thing, it is here.
> Then sense comes; you go to sleep, or have
> Some food, write a letter or work, get something clear.
> Solitude shrinks; you are not all its slave.
>
> Then you think: the bad thing inhabits yourself.
> Just being alone is nothing; not pain, not balm.
> Escape, into poem, into pub, wanting a friend,
> Is not avoiding the bad thing. The high shelf
> Where you stacked the bad thing, hoping for calm,
> Broke. It rolled down. It follows you to the end.

That, of course, like much modern literature, sees man as (so to speak) self-created, spoiling what he might have made of himself. But God isn't totally missing from the scene. Gascoyne, the writer I spoke of a moment ago, goes on to speak of the hand of love that has thrown him down; and there are the great modern Christian writers, Edwin Muir, T.S. Eliot, Norman Nicholson, Solzhenitsyn.

But more generally, God figures quite a lot, though one must admit often in curious guises and under odd names, in modern writing, which yet is overtly secular and at the very least agnostic.

Sometimes, of course, he figures more traditionally in the description of *spoiling*, as, for instance, in W. H. Auden's 'The Love Feast':

> In an upper room at midnight
> See us gathered on behalf
> Of love according to the gospel
> Of the radio-phonograph.
>
> Lou is telling Annie what Molly
> Said to Mark behind her back:
> Jack likes Jill who worships George
> Who has the hots for Jack.
>
> Catechumens make their entrance;
> Steep enthusastic eyes
> Flicker after tits and baskets;
> Someone vomits, someone cries.
>
> Willy cannot bear his father,
> Lilian is afraid of kids;
> The Love that rules the sun and stars
> Permits what He forbids.
>
> Adrian's pleasure-loving dachshund
> In a sinner's lap lies curled:
> Drunken absent-minded fingers
> Pat a sinless world.
>
> Who is Jenny lying to
> In her call, Collect to Rome?
> The Love that made her out of nothing
> Tells me to go home.
>
> But that Miss Number in the corner
> Playing hard to get . . .
> I am sorry I'm not sorry
> Make me chaste, Lord, but not yet.

The unseen powerful presence of God presses there on the poet's
uneasy consciousness.

Perhaps most movingly of all, in this modern sense of dereliction,
there are glimpses of the dereliction of God himself. And I think it

is perhaps curious that of all the aspects of God which the modern writers can accommodate, it is God's dereliction that they find most accessible: not his power, certainly not his authority, but dereliction. Here is a translation of a well-known Latin hymn by, of all people, Samuel Beckett:

> I am not moved to love thee, my Lord God,
> By the Heaven thou hast promised me:
> I am not moved by the sore dreaded hell
> to forbear me from offending thee.
>
> I am moved by thy dishonour and thy death.
> I am moved, last, by thy love, in such a wise
> that though there were no heaven I still should love thee,
> and though there were no hell I still should fear thee.
>
> I need no gift of thee to make me love thee;
> For though my present hope were all despair,
> As now I love thee I should love thee still.

Now that is an unexpected Beckett: and yet the characteristic note of Beckett is present: and it is God's dereliction that has caught his attention.

And that, I suppose inevitably, makes me turn to the other side of the coin. This other pole of modern writing is just as powerful but less accessible. Not as many modern writers, if I can put it this way, are as hopeful – seriously. It is worth noting though that some of the writers I have mentioned – Solzhenitsyn, Saul Bellow, William Golding – all Nobel Prize winners – rise to real hope and real delight set over against the distress of their vision of humanity's dreariness and darkness. For instance, in that same novel that described entropy, Golding's strange, rather clumsy hero suddenly discovers that life is *delight* as well as *duty*, that it is 'Hallelujahs!' And this is how he puts it:

> I tried to tell the boys [he is working in a boys' school] about everything rejoicing as it might be with Hallelujahs and that. But I could not. It is like going over from black and white to colour. There was a bit of sun on a tree over by long meadow and I. The boys went off to music appreciation. I hear hear but only a bit.

So I *left my work* and went after them and stood by the garage
near the music-room window. They played music on the gramo-
phone it came out loud and I heard it like I see the trees and the
sky now and the boys like angels. It was a big orchestra playing
Beethoven a symphony and I for the first time I began to dance
there on the gravel outside the music department window. Mrs.
Appleby saw me and came so I stood. She shouted to me marvel-
lous isn't it the Seventh. I didn't know you cared for music and I
shouted back laughing neither did I. She looked like an archangel
laughing so my mouth shouted no matter what I could do. I am
a man I could have a son. (*Darkness Visible*)

A celebration of life in all its dimensions is there: the physical, the
creative and the eternal: 'Hallelujahs!'

One could also quote from John Wain's lovely poem, 'This above
all is precious and remarkable', where the hope and the delight is
in the recognition that against all the odds, human beings *do* venture
to trust each other and that in the end, against the odds, society
works because of it.

Finally, there are occasional glimpses of the hope that goes beyond
death and the grave and despair. Susan Hill, who has written some
very dark novels, has written one novel of great light as well as
darkness, *In the Springtime of the Year*. It is a simple and moving
account of one young woman's experience through one year, after
the sudden and totally unexpected death of her husband. She goes
to the church on Easter Day. (We must remember that Susan Hill
is not, overtly at least, a Christian.)

The last time she had been inside the church was for Ben's
funeral. Well, she would not brood about that, it was over and
she must think only about this, trying to understand. And she
must go in among all the people and never mind if they stared at
her and judged her. But seeing them walking up the hill ahead,
and a group standing in the church porch, she clenched her hands
tightly, and it seemed that her heart would leap up into her
mouth. 'Oh, Ruth, look! Look.'

They had reached the lych-gate. Jo was pointing. She looked.
Had she been blind last year? Had it looked like this? The church-
yard was brilliant as a garden with the patterned flowers, almost

every grave was decked out in growing white and blue, pink and butter-yellow, and underneath it all, the watery moss and the vivid grass; it was as though all the people had indeed truly risen and were dancing in the sunshine, there was nothing but rejoicing and release. She walked slowly across the turf to the side of the church and stood, looking towards Ben's grave. It was like a sunburst. She did not need, or want, to go nearer.

Jo touched her arm. 'You see,' he said, his voice full of wonder, 'it did happen. It does. It's true.'

'Did you ever doubt it?'

'Once,' he said carefully, 'one time.'

Only once, Ruth realized how close to Ben he was, in his way of seeing and understanding the world; he had the same clear grasp of the truth that lay beneath the surface of things, he saw, as she had only glimpsed once or twice, the whole pattern. They had the gift of angels.

Stepping into the church was like stepping into some sunlit clearing of the woods; there were flowers and leaves and the scents of them everywhere, the altar and pulpit, the font and the rails were wound about with ropes of white and golden blossoms, the ledges were banked with bluebells on mounds of moss, and the sun shone in through the windows, sending rippling coloured lights on to the stone walls, catching fire on the brass of the cross and the lectern. Ruth felt nothing but happiness, she walked down between the high wooden pews right to the front of the church, and looked here and there and smiled, if she caught someone's eye, and did not mind that they seemed embarrassed, uncertain of her. She went into the same pew and for a second saw again how it had been that other day, with the long pale coffin that had seemed to fill the whole building, the whole world.

But what she became aware of after that was not the presence of the village people sitting or kneeling behind her, but of others, the church was full of all those who had ever prayed in it, the air was crammed and vibrating with their goodness and the freedom and power of their resurrection, and she felt herself to be part of some great, living and growing tapestry, every thread of which joined with and crossed and belonged to every other, though each one was also entirely and distinctly itself. She heard again the strange music in her head and her ears, and yet somewhere far outside of them.

She opened her eyes again and saw the flowers and the sun on the walls, and these were real, living and beautiful, she was not imagining them or the joy they gave her, the reassurance; and when the clergy came in and they stood to sing the Easter hymn, she felt for the first time, not since Ben's death, but since coming here at all, that she truly belonged, that these people were part of her life. Everything, everything, she saw and believed and understood, that Easter morning. She knelt. She said, 'I shall never do wrong again. I shall not weep out of pity for myself, or doubt what is true or fail to be grateful. I shall be well. *I shall be well.*'

It is only fair to say that the beginning of the next section is, 'The next day was the worst she had ever known'.

2. How are we to judge?

How are we to judge, in this maze of despair and eroticism on the one hand and anger and passion (some of it spurious) on the other? That is to say, how are we to discriminate?

For instance, I spoke of Osborne's grief and anger. The play that he produced, *A Sense of Detachment*, is as sickeningly pornographic in some of its parts as that pornography which he is attacking, because that is the way he attacks it. How are we to judge?

There are very different views on what is a valid critical perspective. Instead of the traditional, liberal humanist view of objectivity, everything is at the moment critically 'up for grabs'. And so I want to identify very simply some of the ways in which critics at the moment are suggesting that all of us can read literature, and what we ought to use as our criteria.

First of all, there is the traditional view of writing as *mimesis*, as 'imitation'. In other words, good writing means as near a perfect representation as you can get. Presumably, the photograph is the highest form of art by that criterion: truth to nature. This view stems from Aristotle. The emphasis is on the reality of the thing pictured, on how clear a picture we achieve of that which is being described or evoked or created. There is a problem of course. If you are in an age where you are not sure that anything has reality, how can you ever agree as to whether this is a true representation of it?

A second critical perspective sees art and writing as 'pragmatic'. The point of writing is to instruct and delight, and the emphasis is not on the thing described, the content, but on the audience, the readers. What is happening to them? How are they being changed, improved by it? Sir Philip Sidney was the advocate of this view. His *Apology to Poetry* includes a lovely line – 'Right poets are they who delight to move men to take that goodness in hand which without delight they would fly as from a stranger.' This particular perspective is obviously that most supported by everybody who sees literature as a means to an end; so that Marxist criticism would very much embrace this view. So, frankly, does much Christian criticism, as we shall see.

Thirdly, there is the view of literature that is simply 'expressive' of the artist: the point of such writing is not the audience nor the object, but the writer. It is 'the spontaneous overflow of powerful feelings'. It is expressing the flowering of genius. The artist is writing about himself. It is indeed, in this particular perspective, almost a soliloquy; he isn't actually too concerned about the audience: the only audience that matters is the one who writes it. So the emphasis is on the unique genius of the writer. Most young writers strongly prefer this view of literature!

A fourth view of literature sees it as entirely 'objective' – words on a page which have no reference beyond that artifact. What you can learn of the writer, what actually happens to you the readers, and what reference it has to the thing described – all of these are irrelevant. It is simply a composition of words on a page; it is the autonomy of literature. It has an existence in its own right.

Fifthly (this is not a comprehensive list – I am sure there are several dozen others, but these are the major popular ones at the moment) art is seen as something that the reader creates with the writer. Teachers of literature, like myself, find this a very irritating critical view – although students love it, because they can never be assumed to have got their reading wrong, since they are simply creating it with the writer. It is known 'in the trade', as they say, as 'reader power'.

I have deliberately not talked about structuralism at all here because that is in itself matter for several lectures. I would simply indicate that the 'objective' and 'mutually creative' perspectives contribute to the theory of structuralism.

Underlying the whole debate is a question of authority. The question is not only *whose* authority. (Is it the writer's authority over the work? Is it the critic's? Is it the reader's? Is it the authority of the work itself?) Even more deeply, the question is whether there is any authority at all, anything by which we can argue.

To make all this more practical, we ought to try applying it. I have taken a piece of literature which has lasted a long time and therefore must have some powerful qualities to it. It also has the virtue that everybody is familiar with it:

> Mary had a little lamb
> Its fleece was white as snow
> And everywhere that Mary went
> The lamb was sure to go.

Let us take that 'pragmatic' theory, that writing is to instruct and delight. And let us assume that the critic, in this particular case, is a sociological critic with a sociological axe to grind. He would look at the first word and he would say, 'Ah, yes, Mary – the subject clearly is woman' and he would then go on to note that 'had' being the second word, suggested that this was a completed narrative of a tale that was in the past: the action was completed. And he would then go on to the adjective 'little' and the indefinite article 'a', and would note with sorrow that there was only one of these things, and that it was clearly undernourished since it was 'little'. Then he would note that the word 'lamb' has a changing ambience which can in fact nowadays imply a quite improper kind of dependency. He would then look at the second line's reference to cultural milieu. Obviously this line could not be applied to an African culture, since there is a reference to snow; so it must be one of the western cultures. But the words 'fleece' has the implication more of the 'mercantile' than the 'servicing'. And he would then notice that

'woman' in this particular period and society was clearly mobile –
'everywhere that Mary went'. He would also notice that the lamb
was 'sure'. That suggests an era of the past, since there are clearly
certainties in it. And finally, I am afraid, there is a ring of finality
about it because although there is a proposal of fidelity, yet those
lost two words suggest a dreadful fate!

On the other hand, if you were the wrong kind of Christian critic
(I do have a few students in the theology department who do this
kind of thing), you would look at this poem quite differently. You
would take that first word 'Mary' and say 'This is a Christian poem';
and in particular, when you saw that that was lined up with 'lamb'
and 'white' and 'snow' would point out that these are clearly all
biblical images and that this is a poem about 'innocence' and
'redemption'. What indeed does 'to go' signify?

All this is, of course, a critical absurdity! I have deliberately
mocked it; but behind the fun is the reason why readers acquire
such totally conflicting perspectives and views about any piece of
writing: and even so, I have only chosen one of the forms of criticism – the 'pragmatic'.

In the end we have to face the fact that the kind of critic you are,
the kind of reading judgement you apply, depends on your world
view – on what your absolutes are. And this is where we have to
try to tackle the Christian, critical way of reading.

3. A Christian critical approach

What are the characteristics of Christian reading? Let me say first
of all, it is not the task of Christian readers, who root their reading
in the Christian faith, to concern themselves only with the overt
and obvious religious element in the book. That is to presume that
only certain aspects of life are 'holy'. Rather, the job of Christians
in reading and in trying to formulate Christian judgement is to
ponder the scope of values which reading as a Christian can make
available. In other words, Christian reading grows from the kind of
faith, the kind of theology, in which it is rooted.

So what kind of a theology, what kind of 'God-talk', do we root
our reading in? First, I think it is important for us to recognize that

our faith is characteristically *paradoxical*. It can embrace opposites. And when we are assessing and evaluating literature, we must have a base that is as big as that. Our faith is both stable and yet open to fresh insight, fresh disclosure. And that is true of all great literature, which is always beyond any final exposition. With really good writing which is rich in imagery, it is possible often to read it in totally different ways and express, not itself, but what *is visible in it*, in totally different foci.

This can be illustrated by literacy critic Helen Gardner's use of a diagram by the art critic, E. H. Gombrich. It contains two sets of lines, drawn in such a way that, depending on how we see it at any particular time, one or the other predominates. Whichever one can see, trying to see the opposite becomes difficult, but is eventually possible. What we find is that one can never see them both at the same time – however we try switching between the two. They are equally valid. Her point was that the Christian faith is like that; that when you are into Good Friday you cannot see Easter Day, because you are cheating on Good Friday if you can. And when you are into Easter Day, the triumph and marvel of it wipes out the Good Friday. And yet they are both there, both essential to the truth. So, she says, it is with any great art. Therefore our critical base, our world view, must be big enough to take that paradox.

The second element in our Christian theology which provides a firm base for Christian reading is its capacity for *judgement;* critical discernment. This is not censorship (except in the technical sense) but *discrimination*.

Truly Christian judgement of books is never arrogantly judgemental. It never disregards the human cost of making.

When we are reading, we have to work within *our* absolutes, our reality as we perceive it. And our reality must be big enough to include the agonizing of the writer – even if we cannot see why he is feeling agony; the pain he has gone through in making that writing; and also it must allow the detached theoretical judgement which stands back from the work and says 'Yes, ah, but . . .' It has to be big enough for both.

Thirdly, the Christian critic's act of judgement needs to assert some *engagement with truth*. It has to look beyond the writer to the structures within which the writer writes, and beyond those structures to the larger world out of which they are created.

The critic's job, arising from this capacity for judgement is to identify the patterns: the deep underlying patterns, the principles that underlie any work of art.

Another element in our theology which is a proper base for our judgement is the fact that it is *trinitarian*. I mean simply this; that the God we see as the reality on whom we base our judgements is not an isolated God but a God in relationship. And that suggests that art, in the end, should not be an isolated and self-directed thing, it should be addressed outwards. Art that is wholly introverted will fall short of a certain dimension of reality. Christian judgement is a 'right-discerning', and a 'setting right'. One of the things we learn from the Bible is that judging does not mean simply writing off. Judging is discerning truly what is good and what is bad, and then putting it right. That was the Old Testament task of the judge, and it is the message of the New Testament, of God himself.

So Christian criticism and Christian reading which merely diminishes or destroys, which wipes out certain kinds of literature, is not truly Christian. The quality of our literature will depend not on abandoning what we find unacceptable, but on a right discerning of what it is that is unacceptable and a putting of it right. There's a job for Christian critics!

Let me give you an example of the kind of thing I mean. George Steiner has pointed out that our age is an extraordinary example of what he calls 'de-worded man'. In fact he suggests that writers like Beckett actually aspire to a condition rather like that of *aphasia* (severe speech disability) as an expression of man's dereliction, loss of order and loss of articulation. There is a very powerful passage in one of John Osborne's last plays, *West of Suez*, where he talks about how, for our generation, 'Words is going to be the first to go'. One of his most offensive characters has been lounging in and out of the play totally silently, and he suddenly erupts at the end, draws out a gun, points it at the writer (who is the hero) and says: 'Man, I feel real sorry for you lot. We count, not like you. We are people. But not you. You don't understand, because words, I mean words, even what I'm saying to you now, is going to be the first to go.'

What John Osborne is identifying here is the expression of dereliction and grief and anger, not by words but by violence, hooliganism, destruction. Words are useless. Wipe them out! They are the language of civilization.

And the corresponding biblical sign of that is, of course, the Tower of Babel: a very powerful image for our times of language which is disjunct, broken. We cannot hear each other. And yet the noise is extreme. Fascinatingly, of course, the correlate biblical signs for the Christian reader, judging, are Babel and Pentecost. Christians must require of their writers a truth to reality – the larger reality that is not the salve of our culture, that is not narrowed to our culture, not the slave to human folly through all history: but which faces both our contemporary situation and the history of human wrongdoing, steadily and truthfully. It must express them probingly in the context of a larger reality: which insists that sickness, and wrongness and disjunction are not the final truth of the human condition because to speak or write of the human condition is to speak of creatures in the mercy and justice of God, conceived, redeemed and transformed by God. No critical structure, no way of reading, which denies a truth as large as that, is big enough. Whatever formula it uses – God, good, love, grace, delight-enlargement – it must in the end reverence the largeness of the human condition as well as its narrowness: its hope as well as its dereliction. And what better basis for such a critical viewpoint than a faith which looks to the dereliction of God himself, and finds in it the strongest grounds of love and hope for the human race? A faith which sees the Tower of Babel – so much of our contemporary literature – transformed, so that the literature of all the nations in all their languages becomes comprehensible – 'Parthians, Medes and Elamites; residents of Mesopotamia, Judea and Cappodocia, Pontus and Asia, Phrygia and Pamphylia, Egypt and the parts of Libya near Cyrene; visitors from Rome (both Jews and converts to Judaism); Cretans and Arabs – we hear them declaring the wonders of God in our own tongues!' (Acts 2.9–11).

The Self-regarding Image: Television and Video in Everyday Life

by David Porter

Television is a pervasive consumer art-form, different in many ways from those in the rest of this book. It spends much more of its time than they do in communicating information. Television programmes are often created by a team who would not readily describe their work as 'art' in any usual sense. And many more of us are consumers of television than are consumers of theatre, literature, music or any other of the arts. Perhaps because it is a special case in the arts, Christians have always had an ambivalent relationship to television.

Even in the days long before we had any books about 'the Christian attitude' to such things as abstract art and rock music, the question of how a Christian should relate to television was already a problem. It has continued to be so.

1. The impact of television and video on our homes

It's a truism to say that television and, increasingly, video, affect the whole of our lives. I'd like to look at that impact from a number of different aspects.

The Social Dimension

We could begin by thinking of the way in which television has radically changed the way in which we relate to each other. Take, for example, its impact on the family. In 1973, 94% of UK households owned a television. By 1983 the figure had risen to 98%, and 18% of households had video recorders. There is a similar pattern here, for it has been suggested that by 1992, 75% of households

will have video recorders. As an alternative to these cold statistics
let me quote the radio producer and presenter Ted Harrison, who
has calculated that the British spend a total of 80 million man-hours
a week watching television soap operas – the length of time it took
to build a mediaeval cathedral. Certainly many families spend more
time watching television together than they do in any other family
activity.

The Spatial Dimension

In this context we might explore the question, how does television
fit into our living space? There has been a development here. When
television began, many people saw it as a kind of domestic cinema.
Part of the reason was technology. In 1935 Raymond Postgate
thought that to portray facial expressions adequately, the screen
would have to be twenty square feet in area. Though the technology
turned out to be more efficient than that, the early televisions were
console models, often dominating the other furniture and becoming
the focal point of the room. It was part of the wall, like oil paintings
and Welsh dressers, and it turned the room into an auditorium.

Though television sets have become smaller and less imposing
(partly because of the increase in the number of colour sets, which
are cheaper when small), there is still something of that attitude
remaining. Think for a moment of the particular television that you
know best. Where is it in the room? What objects stand on it?
Perhaps there is a selection of family photographs standing on it,
or a particularly valued ornament. Often the video recorder is
stacked neatly beneath, for practical reasons obviously (length of
cables etc.) but perhaps also to display together the two most costly
items in the room.

There is significance in the way that as a nation we treat our
televisions, compared, for example, to the way in which we treat a
radio or a cassette player.

The Dimension of Mobility

But television is not a static element in our environment. And a
quite different set of considerations arises from this. How does
television move around our living space? The past few years have
seen a number of radical changes. A general move towards smaller

sets, as colour has become more popular, has been accelerated by the innovative flat-screen technology of, for example, the pocket television recently produced by Clive Sinclair and the small-tube versions that preceded it. Now that television is portable, it is part of the extensions of our body – in much the same way that the motor car is, as Marshall McLuhan used to say – as well as of our living space, and we can watch television anywhere we like, in the kitchen, the bedroom, or even out of doors.

In addition, video screens have appeared in many areas of everyday life outside the domestic environment, and in a few unexpected guises within it. Television can give you step-by-step advice in cooking, carpentry or gardening. The home computer is usually marketed as a device which can plug into your television, and newer sets have special channels for video and computer input. Some even double by design as domestic televisions and as computer monitors. The use of video in communications, long accepted in airport booking halls and similar places, has been extended to the Oracle, Ceefax, Prestel and other services, all of which use your television as a terminal to a larger database. So television is in the process of becoming a window on to a larger world. Of course it always has been so, but now there are facilities for interaction. You can lean through the window, as it were, and do things. You can purchase goods, bank money, and buy tickets using a television and some simple hardware. In all these, video either on tape or on disc has a role to play as well, particularly in the field of database information technology and its domestic implications.

The result of these developments is that television simultaneously creates its own environment, and also transcends it. In many domestic homes today you can sit in a room which has been defined by the television which is its focal point; and through that same television you can go outside its walls, either in imagination or in terms of verbal communication.

The historical dimension
Colin Morris has recently reminded us[1] that what we receive from television is an artificial memory. In these days of international programme selling it's a global phenomenon. For example, in Japan they watch *Coronation Street*, with Hilda Ogden talking to Percy

Sugden in carefully-dubbed Japanese. One-third of the British population watch that particular soap opera, and possess the artificial memory that goes with it. They know that Deidre was unfaithful to Ken, that the Tilsleys sold their house to finance the garage, that Stan Ogden died in hospital. And the Japanese know it too. In the same way we in Britain share the artificial history of Dallas, as do many other countries. For many people, the characters of TV soap are real people, to whom they can (and do) write letters. Actors playing unpopular characters in *Eastenders* have been attacked in the street. Strip cartoons based on soap characters run in the tabloid Press, and currently, as I prepare this chapter for publication, the actor playing Michelle in *Eastenders* is becoming a television personality as a sort of real-life Michelle, valued not so much for her own intrinsic personal qualities but for her thoughts and reflections on the soap plot – a mouthpiece for the Michelle who for many is the more real person of the two.

Of course it's not just fictional history which television provides. Major historical epics are commonplace now, whether they be sagas of British rule in India, life in an English stately home, or a series like Kenneth Clark's *Civilisation*, Bronowski's *The Ascent of Man*, or Carl Sagan's cosmic epics. On a more work-a-day level the Open University provides many hours a week of history lectures. Video, too, is a valuable tool for historical studies because it can be used selectively and repetitively in a way that television can't.

Language
How strong an influence television has been, not only in our spoken language but also in our use of symbol and concept! Even at the level of spoken words, the influence is remarkable.

When my family acquired a television I was in my late teens. I hadn't seen a great deal of television until then, and was still at the point where many of the American films didn't make sense to me because I couldn't understand the accent. In the community in which I lived I was familiar with several African and Chinese accents. As a Liverpudlian I had had to come to terms with unfamiliar regional dialects (such as BBC English) just to listen to the radio. But I had not had much contact with Americans at all, and found it very difficult to understand them when they spoke.

So I came to television with very little familiarity with one of its major languages. Yet within months I was listening to everyone from slow-talking John Wayne to slick gangsters from New York, and making sense of most of it. And I do not think that my experience was unique.

That's one aspect of language in which television has been influential. But it also exerts an enormous influence on our language of image and symbol. Take for instance the car chase. This is a standard component of a good deal of run-of-the-mill television feature films. How many times on television have we seen cars driven off mountain roads? The image is a predictable one: the car turning over and over as it falls into the precipice. On impact, it explodes in a blazing inferno of flames and smoke.

But in real life, cars do this very rarely. In fact American cars, which feature in most of the precipice-drops we see on television, have strict safety regulations to prevent this happening so far as possible. The Jaguar was refused entry to the USA for quite a time because the placing of its petrol tank failed to satisfy these regulations. Yet television ensures that for most of us, cars are things that explode into flame when they go over cliffs. That is the symbol which television has given us (and which it has itself derived from Hollywood) to represent a reality that is actually quite different.

Take another abiding image of television. How many of us, apart from television, have ever seen anybody die? And yet the 'Moment of Death' is a common element of television vocabulary. We see it in television fiction, of course, but we also see it in news items and reports. But what we are watching is affected by the very fact that we *are* watching it. There are cameras present at these deaths, or we would never see them. Malcolm Muggeridge has described an execution in Nigeria in which the countdown was actually interrupted so that the photographers could reload their film. The condemned man had to wait until the Press was ready.[2]

Both these are examples, out of many others, of the way in which television both extends our symbolic and imagic language, but at the same time can easily corrupt it, by providing it with new but badly-defined terms.

Aesthetics

No consideration of television and video can ignore their impact on aesthetics. This is an area in which television has been very influential, but so has video – and to a much greater extent.

In the case of television most of the aesthetic distinctives are to do with scale. Compare television with the cinema. In the cinema you sit in a regimented row of people, whom you do not know and will never meet. You sit in the dark. The sound system – probably stereo or even quadraphonic – is loud. The images on the screen are larger than life.

Television, on the other hand, is something that you watch in your home, perhaps with members of your family. The lighting is at normal levels, so that you are aware of other objects and other people in a way you're not aware of them in the cinema. There are distractions; the telephone might ring, visitors might arrive, one of the children might wake up and come downstairs to be cuddled. The sound is adjustable to what you (and perhaps your neighbours) want it to be. The film or the programme is contained in a small box, even at its largest only a fraction of the size of the cinema screen. Usually, everything is smaller than real life, unless a close-up is being shown.

These factors have an effect on how television communicates and how it invites us to respond. I don't think it's at all extravagant to suggest that a new aesthetic, a new system of criteria for excellence, has had to develop because no vehicle for the arts remotely similar had ever existed before television.

Some hallmarks of that new aesthetic are for example the emphasis on simplicity of image. In the cinema the screen is full of detail. On television the same films look cramped; indeed, only part of the cinema image of some films can be portrayed on television, so a silent process of editing takes place. By contrast, television images have to make their effect with an economy of detail, because the eye's capacity to take it in, in a small screen, is limited. As a direct result of this, the television image has a limited interest-span, and many programmes rely on kaleidoscopic quick-change images. The use of sound could be similarly examined, and the way in which, for example, the different levels of sound in cinema and television contribute to a distinctive role for sound in each.

In news and documentary, television has the advantages of immediacy. It can show very recent film or live action. The cinema film is made over a long period of time, and watched by audiences for months or years. Television makes much use of instant images which it discards readily.

Television is an intimate medium, frequently interpreting what it is visually communicating. The simple, broad images of the screen are often accompanied by voice-overs or narration. The role of the presenter is a characteristically televisual phenomenon, for reasons which also explain its effectiveness in radio.

Another aspect of television is that it operates as a continuum. You cannot turn it back, and if you miss it one night then the next night will be different (though the video recorder is changing this, as we shall see). Despite the number of television repeats, we are still far from the situation in the cinema, where a film not only occupies a single cinema for a week or weeks, but is also showing at several other cinemas as well. This has social implications – the moment of television becomes very important, and it dominates because it offers a single chance to see what is available – but it also has direct implications for the aesthetic language and image which is used. Television and its viwers are engaged in dialogue, and the things that make that dialogue tend towards banality or excellence – the aesthetic criteria – have to do with the matters we have just been discussing.

Of course the continuum of television has been radically threatened by the emergence of the domestic video recorder and its use for 'time shift'. Such features of the video revolution indicate a quite different aesthetic to that of television. Unlike television, video, like the cinema, is a library of repeatable short segments of communication. If we were to pick out a few hallmarks of the aesthetic implications one of the best examples would be the pop music video.

The formal constraints of the pop video are similar to those that used to apply to the 78 r.p.m. shellac record, when the programming and production of music was conditioned by the fact that it had to fit on a four-minute side. In the same way, a century ago the whole structure, length and concept of the novel – and therefore its aesthetic choices – were dictated by the fact that the circulating libraries would only buy novels that extended to three volumes.

Within the short span of the music video, image is paramount. The quip 'nice video, shame about the song' is significant. The classical composers who set German lieder consistently avoided setting first-rate poetry, preferring second-rank poets; they knew that fine poetry and fine music sat uneasily together, and made the text subservient to the music. In the new aesthetic of video a similar thing often happens, and the reasons lie in the structure, length and formal qualities of the video as a form.

2. Some problems

After that – necessarily selective – survey of some aspects of television and video, and some of the ways in which they affect our everyday lives, I want now to identify four 'problem areas' which, I suggest, present themselves to any Christian who spends time watching television.

Let me begin by suggesting that what we have been discussing is a revolution of form. A long-standing revolution, it's true; John Logie Baird's first experiments took place in 1923, the first BBC transmission on station 2LO was in 1929, and the first public television service was inaugurated by the BBC in 1936. But the growth of television in a domestic environment since then has something of the quality of a revolution by attrition. And as I've suggested, that revolution is in form – in technique, in language, in technology, in format, in structure and so on.

But it is a revolution which is not entirely sure what it is rebelling against. Television, acting sometimes as a window, sometimes as a mirror, reflects the manners and concerns of its period. That is why it dates so much more quickly than cinema. It exists in ordinary homes and speaks often of real people. In cinema, there is a style to be aspired to that transcends ordinary life. Where television behaves like this, I think, it is because it has taken on board the aesthetic of cinema, and is often the loser thereby.

For example, the authentic television aesthetic at its best is well illustrated by a Schools Television production of *Macbeth* which is occasionally repeated. It used stark heads in close-up against black backgrounds and minimal props. It could only have been done on television. Samuel Beckett in *Happy Days*, *Play* and other works achieved a theatrical analogy, but it was only an analogy to what television achieved in this production as of right. It had a quality – an immediacy, a particular kind of internalising of the drama – which couldn't have been achieved in cinema or in any other art form.

In the history of the West, revolutions of form have almost always been symptoms of revolutions of ideas. That was so in the case of the Romantic movement, the French Revolution, and the twentieth century twelve-tone musical revolution, for example. And I think it is fair to say that this on-going revolution of forms which television represents is the mirror or the window that reveals a parallel revolution of ideas.

I choose the word 'parallel' with care. Television is a committee in search of an agenda. In that sense it isn't going anywhere. It has no future, only a perpetual present. Its role is to mirror, to present, to report, portray. Though filtered through innumerable perceptions, it remains the most transparent medium by which we are being made at home in the world in which we live. And I believe that by and large it reports rather than critiques. There is analysis, and that analysis is no more neutral than that of newspaper journalism. Neither is the viewer totally passive in the face of a torrent of television output. Yet substantially, television is an instrument of observation rather than interpretation. It holds, and portrays, the middle ground of life.

As a Christian I have to concede that there are immediate problems raised by this conclusion, and they are problems shared by all the media and vehicles of entertainment. For Christianity is itself a critique of society; the gospel has always stood opposed to unfaith; Christ is ever a name that men reject; the cross is and always has been foolishness to men. That's why I began with a survey of television in some very practical and critical areas, because I am anxious that my first point regarding a Christian view of television and video should not be dismissed as mere pietism. It is simply this. Television presents us with a moral problem.

A *moral problem*

It is a problem shared with tabloid newspapers and popular magazines. Quite simply, television is a bit of an embarrassment to the
Christian. It sits in our homes, prattling away like an O-level parrot,
pouring out a constant stream of inanities and flannel – punctuated
by productions of the very highest quality and content.

At the back of the minds of many of us who watch television, I
think, is a slight feeling of guilt, as if we had a friend who by and
large was vulgar, foul-mouthed and abusive but on occasion could
philosophize like an angel. We might cultivate such a friend to
benefit from his occasional wisdoms; we might even cultivate him
in the hope that in some way or other we might have a beneficial
effect upon his coarser mannerisms, stop him picking his nose in
public or telling filthy stories – but there would still be a great many
Christians to whom, rightly or wrongly, we would be embarrassed
to introduce him; and we might find ourselves indulging in elaborate
self-justification if the vicar called while we were listening to him.

Television faithfully reflects contemporary values. For example,
it reflects current sexual mores. There's hardly a panel game that
doesn't have its quota of sexual innuendo, camp homosexual slap-
stick, and blue jokes. Most of the soaps have plots that revolve
around infidelity in one variant or other, but it is almost always
reported, not criticized. Soap opera involves an interesting balance
between advocacy and entertainment, but the balance of content,
as revealed by an analysis of the themes of most of the storylines,
is squarely in the values of materialism and self-interest.

Other moral standards are reflected in the mirror that is television.
Avarice is reflected in many ways, ranging from the bizarre excesses
of such shows as *The Price is Right* (on the whole, one of the more
entertaining faces of capitalism) upwards. A very large number of
television programmes present a world that is self-contained and
rejects the necessity for a personal God who might actually be
wanting something from mankind.

Concepts such as holiness, discipleship, the centrality of Christ
in the cosmos, and the desperate nature of sin are quite foreign to
much of the world of television. If that seems to be too sweeping a
statement, you should try watching so-called 'family' television with
an eight-year old daughter. Despite recent commendable efforts to

curb televised violence, the Authorities still appear to see no problem in gratuitous innuendo, sexism, racism and many other abuses which appear in early evening light entertainment and go well beyond any 'acceptable vulgarity' which might be considered part of the heritage of the British comic stage.

It's a very broad point, and perhaps an easy one, but it has to be the first one. My intention is not to deny the validity of the representation of man's sexual nature on television, provided it is justified and is portrayed with due constraint (such as are outlined, for example, in the IBA Guidelines). But for the Christian, television presents a moral problem.

It is a problem that reverberates far beyond the area of sexual morals; television is often guilty, for example, of pandering to racist and sexist attitudes, to a taste for violence in popular culture, to an anarchy which is only part in jest. It has created its own unique problems, too; perhaps the most obvious one is the cult of the television presenter. Meteorologists and astronomers with amusing accents can become stars overnight and have their views sought on a huge range of issues. In one sense, this is harmless fun. In another, it speaks volumes about the sense of values which television attaches to personality of a particular kind, a kind which looks good on screen. This concept of an autonomous, self-referring value system culminates, I think, in the idea of 'good television', which can be a quite separate matter from 'good content'. All sorts of issues are raised by this, including the whole moral issue of how we assign worth to things and to people.

A problem of priorities
The next problem is not unique to Christians but has a fundamental relevance to us: it is that television establishes a lordship in our lives.

Television is a transitory medium operating in a continuum. Its images, once discarded, rarely reappear. If we want to catch them we must be in the place and at the time where they are. Television demands a synthetic timetable which you have to superimpose on the normal patterns of domestic life, a different timetable even to that of the cinema which offers several showings of the same material at conveniently varied times of day.

At this point, of course, the video recorder stands opposed to the lordship of television, by replying, 'You can show what you like when you like; but with my 24–day 8–event pre-set timer I will make it possible to watch your offerings at the time that *I* choose.' There is a real possibility that over the next few years our whole viewing patterns will change because of this, and we'll all get to bed a lot earlier. (Though video has its own problems as we shall see.)

So if the Christian contemplating television has a problem in the area of morals, then he also has one in the area of discipleship. Even if, as he must, he submits the lordship of television to the lordship of Christ, how can he allocate his time so that his responsibilities to family, church, friends, work and recreation are properly balanced with the demands of this wonderful and exasperating medium? What is more important – a good programme on the television, or good conversation with friends, or reading a good book?

The answers to these and other questions will depend on circumstances. I don't believe the answers come easy, and one can make many mistakes.

A problem of truth

Perhaps television's biggest untruth is its claim to portray truth. In all sorts of ways it claims to reflect the world in which we live. We are presented with documentaries, news, discussion programmes and informational programmes about a wide range of subjects. This information is communicated using photography, with all that that implies about immediacy and truthfulness. The reporters and presenters are either experts or eyewitnesses, with all that *that* implies about immediacy and truthfulness.

And yet there is an untruth here, though not necessarily a malicious untruth. The untruth rests in the assumption that if you point a camera at someone, you convey the whole truth of what that person wishes to communicate.

But that begs a number of questions. It assumes that the person is being quoted in his or her entirety, or that if not, the most representative extracts have been used. It assumes that the camera angle is a neutral one, neither enhancing nor diminishing the stature of the speaker. It assumes that the presenter will not add his own perceptions to the report by way of comments made afterwards, and that there will be no juxtaposition of that item with others in such a way that the statement made will be qualified or changed by association.

Many of these factors were well demonstrated in the television coverage of the miners' strike, both from the point of view of the police and the union. In the portrayal of pit violence, the placing of the television cameras was dictated by safety and security, and this was a legitimate consideration. But the result was that the image presented was always one of the police being attacked, of miners pressing towards the police. This was, if not intentional, certainly a useful bonus for the case the police were making. On the other hand, numerous television interviews with Arthur Scargill found Mr. Scargill practising his skills as a seasoned interviewee, deliberately filibustering as the end of the interview drew near so that in the crucial last few minutes he could dominate. There were several debates between working miners' wives and striking miners' wives which were allowed to develop into real bitterness so that the arguments were quite overwhelmed in the demonstration of the passions raised by the confrontation. It was valid television to show those passions, but it did mean that the loudest voices were left with the floor.

Television depends on a flow of image, and the juxtaposition of those images is part of how television works; a good manipulation of images is the triumph of the programmer's skill over expediency.

Effective television relies on, and is constrained by, a strong time factor. In one consumer protection programme which relied heavily on investigative journalism, an Asian had agreed to appear on the programme to defend himself against accusations of dishonest business dealings. He had a prepared statement which he insisted on reading. The presenter pressed him to abandon the statement and answer specific charges relating to specific cases. The Asian insisted on reading his statement. The presenter kept repeating, 'Look, you have only a few minutes to justify yourself in front of all these viewers, and you're wasting it.'

The implication was that there was only one way to justify himself. The fact that the Asian considered that his statement would do the job equally well was ignored, and a mounting sense of time-pressure imposed on the defendant. I believe on balance that the programme's case was a good one, though not much debate took place. But what was happening on that programme was as much 'trial by television' as was the classic Frost-versus-Savundra confrontation that first gave the phrase currency – recently given an interesting twist by the 'People's court' shown on British television in both its American and British versions.

Part of this problem is that of the authority which television bestows just by being television – a problem which it shares with other news and documentary media. 'It must be true, because it was on television', is a common attitude. I saw something of this when I worked with Harry Bagnall, the vicar of Port Stanley, as ghost writer of his story of the Argentine occupation of the Falklands. I discovered on several occasions that the facts as given by Harry Bagnall were at odds with the published accounts. But when I checked Harry's papers and other corroborating evidence it was obvious that some inaccuracies had passed into the received story of the occupation, and with the authority of the media behind them the errors have become believed as truth, especially as some of them were perpetrated by well-known television reporters. The fact that errors happened is only to be expected. What is disturbing is the fact that the errors have been hallowed in this way.

I have also seen local communities in the North acquiring their attitudes to Rita Nightingale, with whom I also worked, on the basis of press and television reporting which I knew to be inaccurate, but which was unassailable. Everybody who researches in this sort of area encounters the same kind of thing. In a similar way television can make people think that the Christian faith really is how it is defined by certain clerics with a flair for the media and a theology far from orthodox.

A problem of osmosis

We are exposed to many values, messages and concepts from both television and video, and most of them come by way of what one might call natural seepage.

Consider video, for example. Music video is almost purely image. It has become the fastest-growing force in music in the past two years, and has a crucial role in marketing music. The American television MTV (Music Television) channel plays only videos. In Europe, the Music Box channel operates likewise. A well-produced video often relies on incongruity, on shock, on the fantastic and bizarre. The power of video as an art form was recognized by the launching of the first International Video Festival at San Tropez in 1984.

Music videos share with rock and pop music the fact that by their nature they refuse analysis. You *experience* a video. The elements of colour, of symbol, and of image work together in a highly concentrated space of time to produce an effect which communicates something that transcends the component elements.

But consider the videos of, for example, Frankie goes to Hollywood. *Relax* was a nightmare surrealism, focusing on what appeared to be unendurable sexual torment culminating in homosexual rape. It was enormously popular. They produced at the end of 1984 the video *The Power of Love*, which used nativity symbols stripped of their integrity and allied to words of incredible sentimentality. Or think of Michael Jackson's *Thriller*, which television tactfully fades out after its opening moments. *Thriller* is a fantasy about werewolves, and shows armies of corpses rising from their graves. The atmosphere of this video is very similar to that of horror films and video nasties. And that atmosphere communicates. By repeated playings such videos reinforce the statement that the surreal and fantastic are valid representations of reality. They argue for a basic absurdity at the heart of things. When they invite biblical nativity imagery into their vocabulary they do so only in order to defuse it.

Television advertising reflects this also. There is currently a vogue for a highly-stylized new-wave aesthetic in commercials. An early example was the British Airways golf-on-the moon video, which besides including a component of wild fantasy also has the characteristic synthesized soundtrack and high-chrome production – the metallic echoing cries, for example, now sophisticated, for example, into such campaigns as that of Toshiba's with its 'Hello Tosh, gotta Toshiba?' refrain, or the gleaming fantasy of the Harmony 'Do you dream in colour?' campaign. All this technological advance relies on the manipulative possibilities of video editing.

One could talk for a long time about the presuppositions that underlie many of these videos. Another example one could choose

is televised soap opera, much of which I greatly admire for its skills
of plot, characterization and development. Soap creates small worlds
(in which, incidentally, God is usually irrelevant) and in those
worlds sets people who live out their lives before us. The effect is
profound. When in *Coronation Street* Gail Tilsley was living apart
from her husband, one-third of the population of Britain were either
supporting her or opposing her; by so doing they were sharing in
an ethical judgement. In *Brookside*, wily and selfish Harry Cross
was swindled by a betting shop run by the local gangster, and
thousands of viewers watched a nice exercise in situational ethics –
'the biter bit'.

In the same soap a mother was raped, and the scriptwriters
convincingly portrayed her distress. The viewers learned, perhaps
for the first time, the stress of such an event and the effect of various
attempts to help by family and neighbours.

I believe that for many of us, Christian or not, the soap operas
and other light entertainment are actually opportunities to receive
ethical values and to do ethics, to observe and to share in judgements
and decisions, to endorse or condemn.

The problem, however, lies firstly in the fact that we are not
always aware of the values and the issues being placed before us;
and secondly, that we are usually receiving these values from the
hands of those who are not working in the context of a world that
is under God's sovereignty.

So those are four areas in which I think that Christians have some
problems with television and video, though I am sure there are
many more.

I began by suggesting that television is a window and a mirror.
For me as a Christian the problems of television come to a head
when what we see reflected in that mirror or visible through that
window bears little relation or analogy to the reality in which we
live. The Bible tells me that I live in a world in which God is both
sovereign and interested. It tells me that morals are determined not
by fashion or by the needs of the moment but by the nature of God
himself. It tells me that individuals have responsibility on an infinite
level. It tells me that there is meaning in being a person created in
God's image to live in God's place before him. And it teaches me
above all that the thing that makes sense out of this whole crazy

fallen cosmos is the redeeming fact of the reality of God in the reality of the risen Christ.

By and large television ignores this, with honourable exceptions – I particularly respect Channel 4's *Right to Reply* and the very positive coverage given by all channels to the 1984 Billy Graham and Luis Palau Crusades. And that is why I have given this chapter the title of *The Self-regarding Image*. I have in mind that point when television becomes a window looking out only onto itself, a mirror reflecting only itself; a self-regarding image.

3. So what can we do about it?

I want to conclude with some thoughts about a Christian response to what we have been considering.

Firstly, I believe that we should come to terms with television. Very often Christians have dealt with it simply by forbidding it entrance into their homes. If this is because they are leading such a rich and varied life that there is simply no room or need for television, then that is perfectly reasonable. But as a critical measure I think it is usually a mistake.

Even from the utilitarian point of view, television has practical advantages in terms of news and education. One might even get rather spiritually snobbish and think of TV as a handy guide to non-Christian thought and behaviour, and I suppose that too has some validity.

But there are tremendous advantages which television offers. One of the biggest – perhaps paradoxically – is in the area of the family. Television is much better inside the home than outside it, where children are concerned. We can help them to relate to it instead of postponing the matter until they have left home and may not find guidance so easy to come by.

But that again is a negative point. On the positive side I would want to say that there is so much that is good and creative and beautiful on television, and so much that informs and challenges, that it is a wonderful way of opening our children's eyes to the arts and many other areas and at the same time bringing them up to be able to discriminate.

Secondly, I believe that we ought to fight against the assumptions that television makes regarding its own role in our lives. We should reject the lordship it seeks to claim. One practical way of doing this is to dethrone it. Buy a small portable, and stick it behind the sofa when it's not being used. Use it when *you* want to, and force it to fit your schedules. And we should strive to make it not weaken but strengthen family and social structures, by discussing what we see, not just sitting watching mindlessly. Our kids should see a process of choice going on, that there are values by which one can choose.

Thirdly, there is the special problem of video. Video libraries, besides supplying excellent material, are also almost universally places where a wide range of pornographic material is available. This whole issue is a very sensitive one. How do we allow for the fact that our children's classmates may well have obscene and violent videos, hired by parents, lying around the house and be watching them when the parents are out? I think each individual has to prayerfully work out his or her own approach to the use of video. But one thing is certain. If the kids don't learn to discriminate biblically at home, they may well find it much harder to do so outside, where peer pressure is a very cruel thing.

Fourthly, I think we should use television. We should enjoy it for what it offers, not simply because it is there as a convenient source of information and entertainment. This means knowing what is on offer, buying the *Radio Times* and *TV Times* or by some other means finding out what is scheduled. Half of the problems that we as Christians have with the arts and the media would be solved if we did a bit of prior reading and evaluation before we went to the cinema, turned on the TV, opened the book and so on. For example, Alan Bleasdale's series of plays *Boys from the Black Stuff*, besides being a powerful and mesmerizing drama, would also have made a very good basis for discussion for a group that was thinking about unemployment and Christian responsibilities towards the unemployed.

Fifthly, we should *engage* with television. Because television is a continuing dialogue, it takes note of audience response. There are many examples of how viewers have directly affected programmes by writing to the producers or others concerned. Mary Whitehouse is an example of somebody who has demonstrated that you do not have to be specially qualified in order to have an impact on television. We should also take advantage of every opportunity to participate in 'interactive television', by phone-ins, correspondence to *Points of View* etc., and Channel 4's *Right to Reply*. When the controversial *Jesus: the Evidence* was shown, the 'video box' was very well used by Christians who wanted to join in the debate.

I think that it is crucial that this be a contribution to a debate rather than a hectoring diatribe. We have to abandon the Christian imperialism that demands a platform as of right. Mary Whitehouse claims a hearing not because she is a Christian but because she commands the support of a large body of viewers. We can learn a great deal from the Apostle Paul here, who spent three years in Ephesus and never blasphemed the idol once, according to the Town Clerk. Yet the lecture hall was packed with those who wanted to hear him teach the gospel.[3] We shouldn't be afraid of allowing others to speak. Our society no longer has a Christian majority, and if we want to engage with those who don't share our faith we need to listen as well as speak. The letters which occasionally appear on television from Christians denouncing heresy on the air are usually much less effective than those from Christians who grapple with the issues raised by their opponents in the debate.

In this context cable television presents a situation which will become an increasing problem, in that it emphasizes what is currently, I believe, a major problem in Christian apologetics: single-issue thinking. As cable grows in influence the Church will need to be increasingly aware of the difference between witness and proclamation. A Christian channel, financed by Christian money and drawing its resources from Christian sources (and currently illegal in Britain), tends easily to proclamation. But proclamation emphasizes vertical relationships; it is truth preached to untruth, and truth confronting error. As such, of course, it has great value.

But witness is a horizontal relationship. It means standing side-by-side with those with whom we disagree, and communicating by means of dialogue, praxis, example, and simply being what we are. Television has been well served by proclaimers, but has relatively few witnesses in its midst. It would be a tragedy if the rise of cable television and other commercial opportunites meant that Christians concentrated their efforts into proclamation, single-issue polemics, and confrontational apologetics, while at the same time withdrawing their witness from the debate of ideas which television represents.

And so, sixthly, we should try to achieve a strengthening of the Christian presence in television.   There   are a large   number of Christians working in television (and also in video). They need our prayers and encouragement, and we should also give thanks for the Christian content that is present in many programmes. I might mention here the work – not just the explicitly Christian work – of Norman Stone, a Christian producer whose programme *Shadow-lands*, based on C. S. Lewis's marriage, won an international award in 1986; and the late night *Company* on TVS which is I think the finest television religious broadcasting I know.

But Christians in television also need our voices. They need to have confirmed to the broadcasting authorities that they are not broadcasting into a vacuum, that there are large numbers of Christians who have noted and appreciated the contributions of Christians in television. Everybody likes to have samples of market-effectiveness!

In summary, I believe that the key to making television and video blessings in our lives and not curses is that we should think about them. The idea of 'mere entertainment' is never an option for the Christian. We simply cannot abandon our minds and hearts like that. We have to keep a tiny part of us watchful, ready to question, to discuss it – if necessary to turn the set off.

But how easily that can become a joyless expediency, looking out for the dire and the dangerous, never responding to the many good things on television! No other historical period has had a vehicle of such richness made so available to it, bringing art, science, amusement and information into the home. We should not just develop a theology of separation. We should strive to develop a critical language, by talking together, sharing together; by grappling with the truths and untruths of television and video, allowing ourselves to be enriched by what is good as well as rejecting that which is bad.

If we take that road we will eventually have a true Christian presence in the ideas market-place which is television; both consumers and practitioners, articulate, thoughtful, and above all excited by television, and bringing it into a biblical perspective as part of a rich and joyful life.

That is what I'm arguing for, and that is what I pray for.

Notes

1. Colin Morris, *God in a Box*, London, 1984, p. 25.
2. Malcolm Muggeridge, *Christ and the Media*, London, 1977, p. 64.
3. This crucially important demonstration of apologetics is recorded in Acts 19.

Confronting Theatre

by Murray Watts

1. Apprenticeship

There is a story, doubtless apocryphal, of the late Sir John Betjeman being handed a poem by a Christian writer, with the assertion: 'The Lord has given me this poem.' Scanning the appalling doggerel, Sir John threw it into the bin with the reply, 'The Lord has given and the Lord has taken away, blessed be the name of the Lord.' Such an approach would have a very salutary effect on much of the pious nonsense talked about Christian involvement in the arts. It may be true, of course, that in the heavenly realm the base metal of a bad poem is divinely transmuted into gold, a treasure made up entirely of honest intentions. However, the engineer who built a bridge that collapsed killing hundreds might have a struggle in justifying his good intentions to the Lord. He would need mercy, not an encouraging smile and advice to build as many bridges as possible. Leniency, either on ourselves or on others, is not the best way forward to Christian and artisitic maturity. The role of theatre, and the enormous significance of drama in film and television, mean that artists must be no less rigorous in their training than doctors or engineers: they cannot afford to be ignorant of current developments and practices. In some professions, this knowledge is considered a matter of life and death. In the dramatic arts, it is certainly the difference between artistic life and death.

A good play must stand up to the market-place of the theatre, not simply to the enthusiastic applause of St. Botolph's in Mablethorpe. It must be more than a sentimental Christmas card in a catalogue of slight variations on similar themes. It must define its own space, knowing what has gone before, and attempting to add something of its own. This may sound like a depressingly snobbish attitude, but it holds equally true for the poem, the hymn, the sketch, the mime, the play. What is different? What is special? What makes this unique? These are hard questions to ask ourselves in creating any piece of theatre, which frequently depends upon a degree of surprise and, therefore, of originality for its success.

Potential dramatists can be tamed all too easily by the pressures of their environment, whether political or religious. They need freedom to experiment, but may only be asked to produce propaganda. They need to see a great deal of theatre, to study the best films, to discern the differences between truth and falsehood in an actor's performance, by observing the finest examples of the day; instead, they can find themselves pre-occupied with a narrow conception of evangelism. Thus they are forced to keep their talent safe, and single.

The challenge to every Christian is to multiply his talents. Formal education is one way, but another is to study the history of the theatre. There are few great poets who were not also great readers. Likewise, the best playwrights are keenly aware of dramatic tradition – they know how to use it and depart from it. Originality, as T.S. Eliot observed, is a question of relation to tradition rather than being 'wholly original'. The Christian actors and writers of today need to do much more than read the Bible, pray, and then walk on stage hoping for the best. They need to devote themselves to God and to their craft; they will thus honour God by offering the first fruits – the very best – of their abilities. The strange thing is that much Christian exploration of drama, particularly amongst evangelical churches, has fallen well below the standard set by amateur dramatic societies, which may be good for a laugh at their least accomplished, but at their best can rival any professional company.

This is because the members of the amateur company have a devotion to the theatre. They know and have seen many plays. They love their art, even though they cannot devote themselves to it professionally. Many Christian groups, by contrast, have no particular love or dedication to the art; they are merely intent on 'putting over the message'. In this way, they neglect the skills which are essential to any good communication, at any level, sketch or play. Marshal McCluhan's famous dictum, 'The medium is the message', could be adapted to read 'The message without the medium' for many Christians. The *medium* of the theatre, and all that it involves, is not only a legitimate area of study, it is the very lifeblood of truthful communication. Too often the greatness of God is dwarfed by ineptitude in the arts; his mercy and his love, and the tragic waste of human potential caused by sin in the world, are only dimly portrayed, mere shadowy expressions of caricatures of a world that needs to be observed with the accuracy of a microscope.

There is no substitute for apprenticeship to the theatre, and a willingness to learn the craft, even from those whose religious beliefs are diametrically opposed to Christianity. Christ counselled his followers to emulate the shrewdness and the wisdom of the world, in the sense of understanding human nature. Sadly, the most acute exposures of the human soul are rarely found in Christian paperback testimonies. Far more likely, they will be discovered in the plays and films of those who have observed human beings close at hand. The conclusions of writers, their philosophies, and sometimes the absurdity of the universe they portray, can be contended; here, the Christian will have a quite different analysis of the human condition; but the clarity of vision, the particular details of language and behaviour that generate such dramatic force, these are the instruments which the Christian dramatist must learn to handle with a surgeon's dexterity.

There is something fatuous about trying to categorize movements in the development of 20th century theatre, but at the risk of oversimplification, it is worth offering a few points for study. The few strands unravelled here are given their labels only for the sake of a little extra clarity, to indicate that writers rarely operate purely as isolated individuals. There are some genuine lines of evolutionary descent which are worth noting. The selections are personal, neither authoritative nor exhaustive, but hopefully enough to encourage a wider viewing of the theatre. Many of these writers (though not all) teach us to think about our lives, and the lives of our fellow human beings, as they are, rather than as we would like them to be – an honesty of perspective which is one of the foundations for a Christian understanding of humanity.

Confronting the audience

Henrik Ibsen, the nineteenth-century Norwegian dramatist, cast off the melodramas and pompous verse tragedies of his day to produce a stark realism which still influences much theatre today. This line can be traced through Bernard Shaw, who delighted in upsetting the bourgeois moralists of Victorian and Edwardian England, to Sean O'Casey, who provoked the Ireland of the 1920s with his deflation of romantic idealism. By the mid-twentieth century in America, Arthur Miller's *Death of a Salesman* punctured the self-esteem of a society based on high ideals of personal achievement.

In Britain, John Osborne's play, *Look Back in Anger*, inaugurated a theatre of abuse, rhetoric, recrimination and supremely eloquent despair; his disaffection with the self-image of the British unleashed a savage fury, particularly against the hypocrisy of the middle classes. Tawdry urban settings, harsh language and violent outbursts of anger were the building bricks of this new social realism. Whereas before, in the work of Shaw – and, to a lesser extent, even of Coward and Rattigan – the social commentary was wrapped up in a sparkling apparel of wit, that covering was now ripped away leaving a naked and shivering image of humanity. The wit that remained functioned as a machete, rather than as a rapier.

Other writers developed the tradition in their own ways, Arnold Wesker, more than any other, donating the kitchen sink to our dramatic vocabulary. Some critics recoiled from these unadorned plays, which replaced the cosy hearth and rosy-cheeked peasants of romanticism with the squalid conditions and struggles of working-class Britain. It takes little imagination to see how this type of theatre, reaching its peak at the beginning of televised drama, influenced so much viewing for decades to come. Television writers like John Hopkins and Alun Owen, writing in the sixties, pushed the development further. The recent *Boys from the Black Stuff* by Alan Bleasdale, funny, poignant and accurately observed, is one of the finest examples of the social realism which has found its own voice particularly in television; whilst Barry Keefe's *Gotcha* (part of the *Abide with Me* trilogy), is one of the most troubling and yet compassionate pictures of a frustrated generation seen in the theatre in recent years, rejecting sophisticated dialogue in favour of the inarticulate rage of a 'no-hoper' about to leave comprehensive school.

A *theatre of unease*

There is another line altogether, which interacts with the perceptive social criticism of these writers: a psychological realism. This type of theatre – stressing the tension between appearance and reality – has much in common with a Christian interpretation of experience. The behaviour of characters, even the form of the play, is subordinated to an inner, psychological momentum. Strindberg's plays, *The Father* (1887) and *Miss Julie* (1888) come from the era when Freud was beginning his psychoanalysis, and Edward Munch was painting 'The Scream'. The inner torment of the soul, the disruptive power of the human psyche, is the material of these plays. Social forces are treated incidentally to the personal and – frequently – sexual crises of the protagonists. Many such writers have stood out from their contemporaries, in some senses always alone rather than part of any movement, to produce a kind of dark tragi-comedy of the subconscious. Genet, Pinter, Orton and Bond are all supreme individualists in this respect, all disturbing, unclassifiable, but nonetheless symptomatic of an age of geometric steel and glass buildings whose very purity of form belies the chaos of the psychological dimension within every human being.

It has become a truism to describe Harold Pinter's world in terms of non-communication – the pauses, the hesitations, the broken phrases and banal repetitions – but his theatre of unease is undoubtedly a place where people are afraid to communicate, rather than unable. When asked what his plays were about, he gave the cryptic reply: 'The weasel under the cocktail cabinet'. Much of the comedy derives from the refusal to see the 'weasel', the euphemisms and circumlocutions, the innuendos which – in the work of other writers – would reach an eventual clarification. In Pinter's world, nothing is clear, but in another sense it is all terrifyingly simple. Pinter is regarded by many as the greatest of contemporary British dramatists. He has made poetry out of unlikely material: the inarticulacy of human beings; and, through comedy, has evoked the most primitive dread. Ground one thought secure, or perhaps tried to make secure through clever articulations and speeches in the theatre, now crumbles and threatens to swallow us. The human psyche foretells doom.

Surrealism, imagery and absurdity

Another line, closely allied to the above (Pinter belongs here as well), can be traced from Alfred Jarry's monstrous farce *Ubu Roi*, at the turn of the century, all the way to *Monty Python's Flying Circus*.

It should be no surprise to us that a century of cataclysmic disasters, beginning with the First World War, should have spawned a revolution among artists, questioning all values. Marcel Duchamp signed a lavatory bowl and displayed it as a work of art, whilst Europe drenched itself in the blood of so many futile deaths. What relevance could the icons of the past have to this generation of artists? The Dadaists and the Surrealists juxtaposed images in a wild profusion of absurdity: the collages of Max Ernst, in particular, herald much of the surreal humour in *Monty Python*. The humour of that television series was, in itself, a parody of the absurdly incongruous medium of television which throws up a series of unconnected adverts or programmes in rapid succession. It is hard to make sense of such contradictory information, just as it is hard to make sense of a human life in an absurd universe. Changes in artistic form, and in philosophical perception, influenced the theatre equally. Pirandello's *Six Characters in Search of an Author* broke the traditional frame of theatre to allow authorless characters to invade the stage and insist on receiving an identity. Ionesco's play *Rhinoceros* (1947), about a man trying to live his life in spite of the fact that everyone around him is transforming into rhinoceroses, shares the same disappearing frame: 'social', even 'psychogical' realism, is abandoned in favour of the central image.

Absurdity, of course, ironically implies a crisis of post-Christian identity. How can the universe be called 'absurd' unless by reference to some objective meaning? This gap, left by the disappearance of God, is perhaps most poignantly dramatized by Samuel Beckett in *Waiting for Godot*. Far too much verbiage has been poured out about *Waiting for Godot* and, out of respect to Beckett's own silence about his work, it may be best simply to point to it as arguably a religious play. It is not about God or about morality, but it is certainly about passing the time in the absence of these. It must be seen, more than read, for it is essentially an image. The play should be received like a piece of music which affects on different levels than intellectual analysis can comprehend. The symbolism of Beckett has its own roots in the poetic dramas of Yeats and will always stand apart from other examples of absurd theatre. The symbols throughout Beckett's development as a dramatist continue to reduce to an absolute minimum, rather than to expand in the familiar sense, poetic imagery. His world is robbed of colour, fragrance, sight and sound: it is the diametrical opposite of the Elizabethan theatre which shines like a bright star, giving light to the world. Beckett's world, by contrast, is collapsed in on itself, a 'black hole' drawing the light into the endless void.

Reforming the audience

Such plays have the power but also the narrowness of a hermit's vision. Other writers have developed a different strand altogether in their respective attempts to face the realities of present time. They reject the subjective vision, deeply imbued with the personal cries of the author, in favour of the corporate dimension: writers cannot, in their view, live in a cocoon, freed from political responsibility. What they create either upholds or undermines the social order. So a writer unconcerned with his environment, working out his own salvation or the lack of it, can be termed 'decadent'. He is no better than the historians characterized by Marx, who have merely interpreted the world: 'The point, however, is to change it.'

Bertold Brecht developed theatrical forms which included melodrama, song, parable, satire and cabaret, adapting many techniques from eastern theatre, all to present the audience with a theatre of alienation and instruction. Deep, emotional involvement in the action was deliberately sacrificed to remove barriers from political response. The greatness of Brecht frequently transcends a definition, for he was a poet rather than a politician.

There, is a powerful and always controversial line of theatre emanating from Brecht, which influences a number of British dramatists today. John Arden, John Mcgrath and 7.84, Howard Brenton, David Hare and David Edgar are among several who have – in widely differing ways – aroused hostility from the 'ruling classes' for their radical critique of recent political history. The literary endurance value of their theatre may, in many cases, be regarded as secondary to the immediacy of impact.

Frequently the fringe and 'alternative' theatre companies have been the stamping ground for these disaffected writers of the hard left, many of whom felt betrayed by the diluted socialism of the sixties. Here it should be observed that two-dimensional evangelistic drama is not the preserve of church groups: it may well be found in 'agitprop' theatre companies in many parts of Britain. Such companies share the same faults and the same virtues as their Christian equivalents, producing some of the worst as well as some of the most challenging work in the fringe of the British theatre today. Needless to say, the best work survives by rising above mere propaganda and operates on a number of different levels. The message of the most telling 'committed' dramatists cannot be ignored; drama operates in a political context, it is not divorced from social responsibility, and responses to a play should not be limited to curtain-calls and applause. Legitimately, a play may evoke anger and even repentance. It has a political and in a very real sense, a prophetic dimension which should not be smothered by a shallow notion of entertainment.

Entertaining the audience

Having said that, something must be said about the importance of entertainment in the theatre. It might be assumed from the tone of this discussion, that theatre is – by definition – intensely serious, probably dull, certainly didactic if political, and decidedly un-funny (if ever the newspapers describe a play as 'a bitter-sweet comedy' or the *TV Times* advertises yet another 'uproarious farce' based upon divorce, we must be sure to avoid it). The fact of the matter is, many 'contemporary plays' performed in fringe clubs, or in one-off dramas for TV, are insufferably boring and banal. This has not helped the theatre to be favourably regarded by the general public. However, the great plays of the twentieth century, even when serious in their themes, succeed by virtue of their entertainment of the audience.

Quite apart from this, much contemporary theatre is now influenced by another strand running from Music Hall and Vaudeville theatre, through silent films and Whitehall farces to the present world of television variety shows. Something of the stand-up comic element is present in Beckett, and the double-act of variety is echoed in Pinter. A playwright like Tom Stoppard is famous for his ingenious combination of show business razzmatazz, philosophy and logic. Another master of entertainment (who might well hate to be regarded as serious in any respect, despite the gloominess of his vision) is Alan Ayckbourn, who has adapted the farce to present his comedies of middle-class manners.

In addition to these influences, it must be said that sheer entertainment, unalloyed with any ulterior motive, is a perfectly legitimate pursuit for the Christian writer and performer. This issue is so important that it merits its own book; it cannot be given a proper treatment here. Suffice it to say, that laughter is not a tool to manipulate audiences into serious consideration of 'issues': a Christian comedian would not have to slip Bible verses between one-liners, or hand round pamphlets explaining the 'parabolic' interpretation of his punch lines. Laughter, too, is a gift from God. It is a valuable part of our human identity, our own self-awareness. It is good for its own sake.

Religious drama in a post-Christian age

There are so many different factors that influence playwrights today, that only a few lines of descent have been traced. There is, however, one influence which is of particular concern to the Christian dramatist: the need for God.

It was André Gide who said, 'Without worship, we shrink.' His words, spoken at the turn of the century, have a prophetic ring. *Waiting for Godot* has already been discussed, but there are other writers who have explored the need for religion in the sense of making their own kind of pilgrimage. They do not indicate any particular assumptions of theism or atheism, only a deep sense of yearning. Alongside this nostalgia is a highly ambivalent attitude to conventional Christianity as if, somehow, true religion can only be found in the existential sense; or, perhaps, in some primitive, pre-Christian world of unity with nature. Writers like David Rudkin, Peter Shaffer and Denis Potter have explored religious themes in their rejection of a sterile rationalism. Some of their plays centre on the profound need for religious symbolism, whether as a psychological response to the ambivalence of sex, or simply as a way of coping with the loneliness of being human. Religious rituals, reworkings of conventional themes, these have the effect of creating a post-Christian 'religious' drama.

One of the best known and most moving plays of this kind is Shaffer's *Equus*, about a psychologically disturbed adolescent's worship of a horse-god, a symbol produced by his own imagination. Shaffer admits that he cannot subscribe to any 'rigid orthodoxy', but equally strongly states, 'I would dread living in a world where people were not leavened by the idea of faith.' His latest play, *Yonadab*, turns to the Old Testament to examine the story of the rape of Tamar, first dramatized by the Elizabethan playwright George Peele, in *The Love of King David and the Fair Bethsabe, with the Tragedie of Absolon*. The difference between the two plays is more than a matter of four hundred years, and a marked preference in contemporary theatre for short titles: it is a gulf between an era of faith, troubled by doubts, and an era of doubt, troubled by faith.

Power in performance

Finally, something must be said about the revolutionary development of theatrical forms during the twentieth century. A stress on method, and on liberating theatre from the frame of the proscenium arch, has produced an experimental approach to acting and directing, which has emphasized the 'theatricality' of the medium. Influential productions in the theatre have frequently been impossible to transpose into film or television without losing a great deal of energy generated by the arena of live performance, with all its symbolic (rather than naturalistic) potential. In a certain sense, this movement has been a return to the open theatres and apron stages of Elizabethan theatres, but the development has been more profound. The story of twentieth-century theatre, particularly in recent years, has been, in certain important respects, a transition from 'writers' theatre' to 'directors' theatre', and perhaps increasingly towards 'actors' theatre'.

Stanislavsky (1865–1938), one of the great theorists of the modern theatre, developed 'method' acting, the vital creation of a role by means of accurate observation and psychological intuition, and this emphasis on performance has influenced a generation of actors, inspiring creative independence. The actor is not a mouthpiece for the writer; he can, in fact, (as the Polish theatre director Grotowski has pointed out), dispense with the writer. Antonin Artaud (1896–1948), a French director and playwright, advanced the theory of a 'Theatre of Cruelty', which relegated dialogue to a subordinate role and bombarded the senses of the audience with light, sound and gesture, thus liberating the power of the sub-conscious to respond to the mythic element of theatre. Many directors, including Peter Brook, were influenced by his theories. One of Brook's most famous productions in the 1960s was Shakespeare's *A Midsummer Night's Dream*, which freed the comedy from the glass cabinet of literature and the weighty traditions of Shakespearian theatre, swept off the dust, and – with the aid of trapezes, stilts, acrobatics, bright colours, and brilliant ensemble playing – thrilled audiences with a virtual rediscovery of the magic rite belonging to the youth and innocence of the play.

It is impossible to speak of this kind of development without incurring the danger of a kind of 'key facts for O level' approach, but any person seriously wishing to understand the theatre, particularly in its most recent developments, must study the performances and the productions, as much as the plays. The Royal Shakespeare Company's production of *Nicholas Nickleby* demonstrated the excitement and power of a purely theatrical approach, but the inquirer can go further. The work of Eastern European directors such as Lubymov and Kantor, as well as the recent work of Peter Brook, shows theatrical genius at work.

2. The freedom of the theatre

Dissidence
The ritual power of theatre is rooted in the religious origins of the art form. Theatre, by its nature, can touch the profoundest spiritual needs of the audience. Along with some of the arts, this involves not only the formal power of the medium, but also the capacity to offer a radical diagnostic. Theatre, at its purest, can remain free from the communications revolution and, in a certain sense, 'poor'.

Limited to small audiences, to 'those who have ears to hear', it will often run counter to the many other forms of dramatic entertainment possible. At its most enduring level of achievement, it will be fundamentally avant-garde in a way that television drama rarely is. Just as Ibsen portrayed a crisis of confidence, which gnawed at the roots of bourgeois society in the western world – seeing municipal corruption in small towns, and domestic hypocrisies, as dark forebodings of our future civilization – so the contemporary dramatist can question his audience, can redeem its conscience. This was, undoubtedly, the aim of Arthur Miller's great play, *The Crucible*. It remains a potent warning against all forms of hysterical witch hunt, political or religious. It spoke to a society that hid spiritual unease beneath shallow confidence in the status quo, a society that produced the first hydrogen bomb in the same year that it was running scared of writers and poets, condemning them as 'un-American' for this political dissidence.

Many of the great plays of the twentieth century have been of this order, for theatre still has the edge on television for editorial independence. The significance of this can readily be seen in any society with predominatly state-controlled media. Black South Africans have spoken of their rage in township theatre, Athol Fugard has examined the workings of Apartheid through theatre, but the South African Broadcasting Corporation remains a bland medium, thriving on Dallas, Dynasty and political indoctrination. Clearly, theatre does not have such a well-defined 'dissident role' in Britain, but many contemporary playwrights would argue that this is precisely its function. Political dramatists have been quick to see this. Those with deep religious convictions may also find that, denied a hearing in an increasingly arid and materialistic medium of television, the theatre offers the chance for a genuine counter-culture. The Church must take note of this, because it may not be driven underground, as in some parts of the world, but its freedom of speech, its power to challenge prophetically, may depend upon theatrical forms.

Influence
Theatre has the additional task, therefore, of disseminating ideas which, in due course, influence the other media. The economics of

film making make risks extremely rare, whereas theatre can and must take risks. Some of the most powerful screen dramas are dramatizations of novels or plays which have had an existence outside the hothouse of commercialism.

Apart from this indirect influence it may be an irony of the future that the development of cable and satellite in the coming twenty-five years will not diminish, but enhance, the importance of theatre. Although theatre is the poor relation of both television and film, its very poverty makes it attractive to a fragmenting system of communication. The multiplication of channels may lead to the atomizing of the national audience and the intensified search for cheap, home grown products in the regions. Little theatre companies working in schools or youth clubs may find themselves approached by cable channels in the search for the local market. The do-it-yourself element of fringe theatre may be one of the ways churches come to have a more direct and more localized influence through television.

Emotional power

It must be stressed, however, that even if theatre never has any appreciable effect on the other media, it has an indubitable value in itself. It can speak to our visually literate society, which no longer listens to sermons or reads books. More important, the very humanity and directness of the art form may well move people at a time when preachers cannot touch the emotions, since many of them seem to be out of touch with the agony of their own society. Equally important, since one of the vital functions of theatre is to refuse to simplify human experience, good plays may serve as an antidote to the cultic element that threatens to invade Christendom. The legalism, systems of achievements, formulas for righteousness and naive analysis of suffering and analysis of the human condition: none of these belong to the gospel of Christ, nor would they thrive in the best theatre, which is essentially an arena for conflict.

Concentration and the will

The very nature of theatre – live entertainment – is another reason why it should be highly prized by the Church. Theatre requires an act of volition: an audience must arrive, and stay, for a performance.

It must concentrate on the action to a degree that is rare in television. Apart from eating sweets noisily, blowing noses or fumbling for glasses in handbags, the activities which can be simultaneously undertaken are limited.

Theatre, which begins by a mutual act of volition, audience and actors engaging together in the live performance, has great potential for inspiring further acts of the will – decisions to reflect on or discuss what has been seen, or even an opening of the heart to forgotten depths of sorrow, righteous anger, penitence, passion or joy. This is not to say that television cannot have a similar degree of audience involvement but it is very much more vulnerable to interruption and diffusion than the theatre.

Naturally, cinema and the theatrical release of films is a much more protected environment for audience response, but increasingly the cinemas are under financial strain in competition with video, particularly in a country such as Britain which has the highest ownership of video cassette recorders in the world (1 in 4). Despite the remarkable boost to cinema audiences in British Film Year, the long-term future may mean that films may not be watched with the same degree of occasion or commitment. The theatrical environment, whether a cinema or a theatre, encourages concentration on the part of the viewer – and, arguably, produces a significantly greater effect, both on the memory and the will.

3. Freedom from restraints within the Church

Many writers, directors and actors recoil at the notion of censorship, with some justice. It can so easily become arbitrary, and it can lead to laughable inconsistencies, as well as serious repression of artistic freedom. Freedom of expression in the West is a precious gift which, although undoubtedly abused, enables the dissident writer to speak out without fear of repercussions and the film-maker to challenge the ethos of a society by positive contribution. One film or play that has artistic integrity is worth a hundred acts of censorship in its power to offer an alternative. In this sense, the finest work condemns the mediocrity of pornography.

It is fair to say that certain legal restraints must go hand in hand with sufficient freedom for artists to offer a radical critique of their society. Their techniques will vary, ranging from satire to tragedy, from poignant love stories that touch a universal chord to political parables that speak in uncompromising terms to a precise context. The artist cannot wage war without his armoury and there are those in the Christian community who would have him enter the battle carrying an acoustic guitar and a book of simplistic choruses; such is the highest view of artistic communication in some quarters, where the Devil is expected to quail at the sound of a tambourine and a three-point sermon to the faithful rather than at the effective invasion of his domain by the finest communicators.

There is, then, another kind of censorship, and it is the restrictions created within the church by pious sensibilities. All too easily a certain type of Christian is shocked by reality. Dance that recognizes God-given human sexuality is suppressed in favour of long floating dresses and ethereal arm-waving, and music degenerates further and further away from the days when the greatest composers filled the churches with their glorious visions of Christ's majesty or inspired whole generations of believers to meditate on his sufferings and weep at the sadness – the rightful penitence and suffering – of the road to Calvary. If this self-censorship, perhaps more than anything influenced by a generation of television adverts and hard-sell communication (where human experience is edited into brief spurts of propaganda), has arisen in the church's understanding of the arts, so too there is a censoriousness towards the artist working in the world.

Many a Christian artist has drifted from fellowship, discouraged by the misunderstanding and misinterpretations of their efforts. Their freedom is often called in question. The artist becomes more legitimate the nearer they approach evangelistic communication, in fact, the more recognizably functional their art becomes. When it has no clearly identifiable function, as in the case of an abstract painting, it mystifies; when a play is open-ended, refusing to pass judgement' or offer a clear moral, it becomes sub-Christian in the eyes of the zealous. Such people would seize the arts and use them like blunt instruments to club the secular mind into submission: in actual fact, the sincere agnostic is repelled by such transparent manipulation.

So where is the vital freedom for the artist to explore his whole territory, when their Christian brothers and sisters are all too ready to write abusive letters if the artist steps out of line, using a word they do not like, using humour which they do not understand? The author has received various charges of blasphemy over the years, in most cases because of satirical material written out of the deepest Christian convictions. Such responses do not discourage, but they may sadden, and they may widen the gap between the conscientious Christian writer and performer, and their church support. In one case, certain Christians objected to a play produced by a Christian theatre company, treating the relationship between belief and mental instability. To show a person (an historical figure) who was undoubtedly a sincere believer, but landed up spending nine years in an asylum for the criminally insane, upset some people who felt that it was disloyal to God to show Christians in their pity and their human frailty. Several Christian supporters of the theatre company hinted that they would withdraw financial support if the company did not return to what they considered to be a more faithful proclamation of the gospel.

This is an insidious censorship, because it is deeply sincere. Like an invisible ink, it suddenly appears when the heat of debate rises. As soon as there is controversy, and as soon as a work of art is seen as potentially damaging to a successful public relations campaign for God, the protestors marshal their complaints, if not threats. But if Christian artists do not speak the truth at all times, especially when it is most costly to themselves and their own self-esteem, how can they be trusted to speak the truth when literally proclaiming the gospel of Christ? If artists censor their imagination and restrict their work to acceptable subjects, then they enter a conspiracy against the audience. Experience shows that most people have sensitive noses for such deceptions. They can sniff out a charlatan. They will recognize, in due course, the difference between the cult-member with the glazed eyes and rehearsed speeches, and the men and women who offer their very own selves. This was St Paul's definition of his ministry: 'We offered not only the gospel, but our own selves'. The Christian artist can do no less. For better or for worse, he must have freedom to open his heart.

The same kind of misguided censorship was at work when some

Christians objected to the first showing on British television of the
pictures from Belsen, claiming that they were 'obscene' and not fit
for public viewing. Certainly, they were obscene, but in a very
different sense from the way the word was used. Those pathetic
naked figures, with their haunting eyes piercing the viewer with an
unnameable dread, those piles of bodies thrown limply onto refuse-
tips: these were obscenities against God and man in his image, and
they had to be seen 'lest we forget'. The context of this original
showing was a *Panorama* programme in the sixties, surely a legitimate forum for facing up to the truth that this was the darkest
hour, rather than the finest, in all human history?

The petty censorship of our self-righteousness does not do justice
to the Christ who 'knew what was in the heart of man'. Our fears,
sometimes, shorten that list of horrors. Perhaps it is because we
cannot look into our souls without revulsion. The censorship from
within rises up and edits our own conscience, producing a world
view that is – in effect – more like a parish magazine than a novel.
Artists need understanding of their freedom, which they may abuse
along the road, but they do not need red pens circling their every
other word. They need financial support, as much when the patron
is disturbed by a work of art as when he is in broad sympathy.
They need belief and trust, not advertising commissions to promote
a party line. They need to pour out their alabaster jars of ointment
at the feet of Christ, without accusations that their art serves no
useful purpose and should be re-directed for evangelism.

As for the artists, they must submit themselves to the Holy Spirit,
to patient and long meditation, to the art of hearing the still, small
voice and obeying.

A vision for the present: freedom to act
One of the easiest things in western society is to discuss the future.
In fact, the twentieth century is neurotically obsessed with the
subject. Science fiction and horoscopes are not the only evidence of
this futurology, nor is the eschatological emphasis in certain churches and cults. There is the more insidious mortgaging of our
present, for the sake of some imagined future. We take certain
decisions now, accept certain constraints or compromises, for the
sake of our 'career'; politicians beguile the public with five-year

plans; ideologies offer revolutions now with the prospect of future liberation. Against these frequently forlorn hopes in the future, is the opposite reaction of living for the moment, without fear or reflection on the consequences, an epicurean reaction to the gloomy prognostications of atomic war.

The prophetic task in this society must not be confused with the latter day incarnations of Nostradamus, whether they be gurus or sociologists, evangelists or astrologers. The prophet, in the biblical sense, is not simply someone who predicts the future, but someone who accurately interprets the present. In this sense, theatre can have a prophetic role in society. In direct proportion to the accuracy of its interpretation, it may also fulfil the traditional prophetic role of predicting the future. The point, however, is to live now. Christ adjured his followers to live in the present – vigorously and realistically for the day at hand. 'Let tomorrow look after itself.' Can this advice be taken seriously in a futuristic age? If it is not, it is certain that we will waste our lives and, ultimately, abandon the salvation of our souls. The saints knew something of the immediacy of God, the present tense of the spiritual world. They did not allow worries to cloud their vision of a God who stood right in the midst of the hours, minutes and seconds of daily living. This freedom of the moment was, paradoxically, a training for all future realities; without it, they would have been like the majority of humanity, helplessly vulnerable to future disenchantment.

Why is this so important to our understanding of the theatre, and, conversely, to the relevance of theatre to our spiritual welfare? Not least because theatre – even more than other art forms – is concerned with the present tense. It is always present, even if dealing with a wreckage of past errors or the pressures of the unknown: it is always about people living their lives, reacting to their fate or their predicament, now; and for the audience, the now of the actors is also the now of their lives, too, as they are simultaneously engaged in mind and body, presenting themselves in the arena of conflict.

The critics sometimes talk of 'magic' in the theatre: usually, they do not mean literal tricks, or even theatrical inventions, so much as the encapsulation of truth in a performance, a breathtaking moment shared by all, a fraction only perhaps, as shortlived as a bird hovering in flight and then vanishing, leaving the image of flight in the mind. What has taken place is something impossible to analyse, but in a very real sense it is the fruit of a relationship, personal rather than abstract, immediate rather than secondhand. The author speaks, rather than 'has spoken'. The play breathes rather than mechanically records its message. The audience are treated as people rather than as ratings.

There are too many possibilities, far too many, to define the prophetic task of this present tense art form in our society. The diagnostic function has already been mentioned, but there is another which must be mentioned as a counterpoint to this. There are economic, social, and technological reasons for the crisis in contemporary theatre, but there is also a spiritual vacuum which may – in itself – have contributed to the dwindling audiences. There is a hopelessness of vision, even in the best comedies, which afflicts the age. There is a melancholia, or what the mediaeval writers called a state of 'accidie': a despair, amounting to lethargy, an almost total anaesthesia of the soul. Such a state was then regarded as a mortal sin. If it is not a sin, this lassitude, threatening to pollute our world, is certainly a mortal sickness. The task is not simply to expose the affliction but to offer the remedy of Christ. This is not a plea for evangelism, but a plea for the whole truth. Saint Paul knew this when he chose to conclude one letter with the greatest emphasis of all: 'Finally, brothers, whatever is true, whatever is noble, whatever is right, whatever is pure, whatever is lovely, whatever is admirable – if anything is excellent, praiseworthy, think about such things.' (Phil. 4.8.) The task of the Christian in the theatre must be to discern goodness, as well as evil: for what meaning can evil have without such a clear barometer?

The contribution of the Church to our culture is needed even more than it was in the era of the mystery plays. It is needed to revive and inspire. Yet the praise of good, without a foundation of realism, so easily leads to sentiment. Christian bookshops, with their bookmarks, posters of furry animals and Scripture texts, and pantheistic record covers, are a dreadful reminder of what happens when Paul's great list is trivialized and isolated from the world we inhabit. Designers, actors, dramatists, musicians, directors, all have a part to play in liberating men and women from these false images of God – pious stereotypes – and also from false images of man, without hope and without salvation, arising from the work of some contemporary dramatists, for it may well be that the prophet who wrings his hands in anguish at the ruins of the temple, but has nothing else to offer humanity, is a false prophet.

The Christian hope is sure. God has not left the world which he has made, nor changed his mind that it was very good. He has not left us marooned on our planet, struggling to climb up some spiritual staircase to meet him in a remote heaven, nor condemned us to puzzle out our own destiny. He has made himself known through the things that have been made, he has walked with us, even through our most broken-down places on the earth; above all, he has made the devastated human heart his dwelling place. He has not only redeemed, he is also restoring creation to its former glory. In the light of this certainty, the prophetic task of theatre becomes clearer. Freedom in Christ produces a spirit of dissidence, a defiance of contemporary assumptions.

There may be a long way to go before Christians, either individually or corporately, make a lasting impression on theatre at the end of the twentieth century, but it is right to pray and work for this. We should strive, alongside theatres of absurdity or despair, to lay the foundations of a theatre of protest which, paradoxically, is a theatre of joy.[1]

Note

1.   The text of this chapter is much expanded in: Murray Watts, *Christianity and the Theatre*, Edinburgh, 1986.

Making Paintings

by Peter Smith

To confess that my system of priorities begins with loving God and my neighbour as myself is to admit that painting is not the sole object of my desire, nor its progress the ruling principle of my life. But my refusal to idolize the visual arts does not mean that my participation in them as a Christian is necessarily half-hearted. To pursue one's calling and develop one's gifts in service to Christ is to treat them with the utmost seriousness, even though they are held onto lightly as part of life rather than life itself. In our present circumstances, individuals who are trying to develop whatever gifts and abilities they have within a Christian framework will find themselves pulled in many directions. The painter is no exception.

There are still those in and out of the Church, who find it difficult to regard making paintings as anything more than an interesting hobby. Our painter will find himself thrown into periods of self-examination by friends with respectable theological credentials who expect clear and explicit messages to be present in his work at all times. 'It's only a picture of a vacuum cleaner. What is Christian about that?'

At other times he will feel browbeaten by those who see contemporaneity and acceptance by a certain section of the prevailing art establishment as a sure sign that his paintings are good. With the best of intentions, such people want him 'successful' irrespective of the integrity of his work; as though that kind of sucess somehow authenticates the validity of the Christian faith. The current commercial gallery system is a potential market for a Christian's work. Though drawn to its possibilities, he will also be repelled by many of its attempts to control the work of artists by a system of values ruled by commercial interest and transient fashion.

At the present time oil painting is again in favour. But there are still cat-calls from certain quarters that 'painting is dead', having been overtaken by the new techniques of photography, film, TV, and video.

In the face of these and similar attitudes which are equally discouraging, the painter may be tempted to retreat into isolation. He may begin to treat with disdain those who seem unable or unwilling to view his problems sympathetically. No matter how justified this may seem as a response to such difficulties the Christian is not free to solve his problems by a retreat from neighbourly service. C. S. Lewis reminds the artist that as he thinks of his rights he would do well to consider his responsibilities: 'In the highest aesthetic circles one now hears nothing about the artist's duty to us. It is all about our duty to him. He owes us nothing: we owe him "recognition", even though he has never paid the slightest attention to our tastes, interests and habits.'[1]

In this chapter I shall be assuming that, for those Christians so gifted, professional involvement in the visual arts is a valid preoccupation. My interest is in the problems associated with being a painter and the making of paintings. Society provides differing models of the painter and his role, and some are being more helpful than others. Perhaps the Bohemian, rebel, avant-garde image of the painter is the model most deeply rooted in popular imagination. It still permeates the thinking of many who would reject its grosser aspects.

A recent British television advertisement for non-drip emulsion paint cleverly draws on this popular image. It concerns two painters. One is a painter/decorator and the other is a painter/artist. The decorator turns up to paint the artist's studio. They both begin to paint. The decorator, looking very pleased with himself and with a great sense of purpose, gets on with the job efficiently. Meanwhile the artist, in a world of his own, begins to throw paint furiously and randomly onto a canvas which lies on the floor. Once, in his frenzy, he bumps into the decorator and almost knocks over the tray of emulsion paint. By now the decorator is half finished and the artist is busy dragging a bicycle over the wet paint on his canvas. In the concluding scene, the decorator, without a paintmark on him, leaves a beautifully painted room. It is a craftsman's job, well-planned and successfully completed. As he goes, the artist, who by now is spreadeagled across his canvas and himself covered in paint, looks up and says, 'I hope you haven't left a mess!' The artist is deep in an unprogrammed, random aesthetic process. The advertisement is light-hearted with simple stereotypes as characters, but it does depend, for its success, upon the wide acceptance of the Bohemian rebel view of the painter. He is seen as a lawless, eccentric, unconventional, misunderstood, irrational, emotional figure.

Why should this model be attractive to someone who is working within a Christian framework? The answer may lie somewhere in the earlier stages of the development of these ideas. In their book about the artist's image, Kris and Kurz say:

> The new image of the artist which evolved in the sixteenth century found its clearest expression in the opinion that 'wonderful and divine thoughts' come into being only when ecstasy complements the operation of the intellect. This is at the same time a reminder which leaves no doubt that artistic creation rests upon inner vision, upon inspiration. Thus, inevitably, there emerged an image of the artist who creates his work driven by an irrepressible urge in a 'mixture of fury and madness' akin to intoxication. This idea has its roots . . . in Plato's theory of art; but it was not until the Renaissance that painters and sculptors were credited with possessing genuine ecstasy. Thus transformed into 'the stylus of God', the artist himself was honoured as a divine being.[2]

We tend to use the word 'inspiration' in day-to-day conversation rather loosely. When faced with a problem to which there seems no solution, we suddenly get a 'flash of insight'. The Renaissance idea seems to imply more than that. The artist was seen as the pencil of God. A pencil does not draw of its own accord. The one who holds it draws. The work of the artist, the genius, becomes, in a sense, God's work and revelation. The painter is seen and venerated as a kind of prophet, who in his art, from the depths of his soul, literally guided by God, reveals Truth.[3]

One can understand how such artist demi-gods were considered, and considered themselves to be, a race apart from mere mortals. Their divine calling implied that the norms which apply to ordinary people did not apply to them. It is interesting to note that as these ideas took hold, so complaints began to emerge about the unreliable behaviour of artists.

These ideas reach us in a secularized form. The artist is seen as someone who is a law to himself. He is even believed to have an *obligation* to reject all traditions, norms and conventions. He is a revealer of some special kind of truth, knowledge or insight. He creates new, original worlds from his innermost being. If we have removed God, who or what replaces him as the guiding spirit? For some, the artist is one who uniquely expresses and reveals the spirit of his own times. For others, all painting is autobiographical with the painter expressing himself or revealing his own subjective states of mind. There are those painters who surrender themselves to random forces in the belief that chance and irrational activities will provide access to deeper realities. Many artists have long since abandoned the making of objects in favour of staging events or making prophet-like gestures in which events and situations are created to shock or awaken a complacent mass. Aesthetic experience via works of art is pursued for its own sake in the belief that it is a redemptive or spiritual experience. As Flaubert wrote, 'Humanity hates us; we do not minister to it and we hate it because it wounds us. Therefore we must love one another in Art as the mystics love one another in God and everything must grow pale before that love.'[4]

There are many variations on these themes but we need to return to the question posed earlier. Why should a Christian find these formulations attractive? He may come to the conclusion that because secularization has removed God from them, a solution can be found by putting him back. There are many precedents where Christians have tried to baptize paganism but have not succeeded. The problem is more acute for those Christians who are susceptible to certain current theories concerning the nature of God's guidance. They would argue that their paintings are created under the direct and immediate inspiration of the Holy Spirit. They were simply a submissive tool in his hands. It is not surprising that work believed to be produced under these circumstances is often regarded as being beyond criticism. For these painters it is of no consequence if their work fails to reach those standards by which we attempt to evaluate a work of art and determine its varieties of success or failure. It must be right because it, maybe, serves other 'useful' ends. In these circumstances all conversation ends. There can be no effective discourse whereby the work can be evaluated or the artist helped to refine his skills. These things are irrelevant because, being inspired, the work *must* be right.

This is not to deny that the Christian, in this walk of life as in all others, must earnestly and prayerfully seek the help and guidance of God. It is the nature of that help which is questioned here. We enter into pagan ideas about inspiration if we begin to talk about a Christian being possessed, in an uncontrollable, ecstatic way, by God. Those occasions in the Old Testament which speak of the direct inspiration of God do not describe it in 'inspired genius' terms. Bezalel and his assistant Oholiab were especially filled with God's Spirit to make the Tabernacle (Exodus 31.1–11 and 35.30–5). We do not see Bezalel's work described in terms of a demi-god creating new worlds. We see a skilled, knowledgeable and imaginative individual carrying out a certain programme which God provided for him through Moses: an artist/craftsman at work. While we can draw some inferences from these events there can be no easy jump from then to now. Bezalel was at work in the Old Covenant culture and setting. There was a very specific, one-off aspect to his task. In the New Covenant, in Christ, we have no tabernacle, temple or priestly ceremonial. Whatever else we learn from Bezalel we do see that there is no hint of the 'divine madness' about him. His direct inspiration for that Old Covenant task cannot be taken in any simplistic way as normative for the individual artist/craftsman today.

We believe that God will help us and give us understanding as we use the gifts that he has given in his service. This does not imply any direct inspiration which removes from us the burden of responsibility for our actions or the possibility of failure.

If we reject a baptized version of the avant-garde along with the absolute freedom demanded by its inspired prophets, where do we turn? Instead of paintings being the outpourings of an inspired individual maybe their primary use is the transmission of ideas?

During the last decade an interest in the visual arts by churches not previously noted for such interest, lies in part with their realization that paintings have meaning. Nicholas Wolterstorff calls this the Protestant view, which, he says 'rightfully and forcefully calls

to our attention . . . the presence of a world behind each work of
art of which the work is an expression. Works of art are not simply
the oozings of subconscious impulses; they are the results of beliefs
and goals on the part of the artists' He warns us, however, that
'The work by no means always fully reveals the world behind it.'[5]
In other words, while the expression of a world-view is part of the
reality of a painting, the work may not simply be reduced to that
function.

It is usually those who wish to control or manipulate messages
via works of art who highlight this aspect of a painting. The motiv-
ation may be political or religious. It may be a need to manipulate
consumers. We may simply have a burning zeal to share our
particular message. Whichever it may be, once the pressure is there
to make a painting 'message-orientated' there is a strong tendency
to undervalue or ignore the reality of a painting as a painting. This
is no new problem. The Second Council of Nicea in AD 787 said:
'The making of paintings shall be determined not by the invention
of the painters but by the principles laid down by the Catholic
Church'. In these circumstances, the fact that a painting may have
complex multiple meanings makes the activity potentially
subversive. All those totalitarian regimes of left or right make
attempts to control their painters and artists.

This model, which sees the painter as one who visually communicates messages, can seem an attractive one to the Christian seeking
justification for his work. Internally he will have a desire to share
the good news of the gospel. Externally there may be those in the
Church who see his gifts as only of use in that particular way. We
face the danger here that all painting by Christians will be reduced
to a kind of religious advertising.

The reality of a 'world behind the work', important though this
insight is, if taken as the only element in a work of art, will tend
to reduce paintings to slogans. Individuals with important messages
tend to festoon themselves with badges. Often the value of that
which is labelled is lost, overwhelmed by its convenience as a slogan
carrier. For those with overriding commercial interests the world is
a useful hoarding on which to paste false dreams. For those whose
ambitions are political, it is a useful pinboard to hold its posters.

The Christian dare not reduce his experience of the world to raw material for tracts. A painting is more than a diagram of a particular view of life. Unfortunately, we are inundated by visual depiction the function and intention of which is the transmission of simple messages. This is not to condemn universally such visual depiction as bad. The process by which immediacy is achieved is often complex. The simple messages may have many not-so-simple implications. They may be of such quality that they become valued in their own right long after the initial message has become redundant. Nevertheless, such visual depiction, in the main, is subservient to, for example, the consumers' speedy and easy assimilation of the advertisers' slogans. While some paintings in recent years have made the advertisers' depictions of human experience their subject matter, vast numbers of painters do not operate in that way. Our habitual reaction engendered by familiarity with visual slogans and immediate responses, is inadequate when faced with paintings whose disclosure can only be experienced over a period of time.

Many artists, having realized that paintings are no substitute for the verbal preaching of the gospel, have still found themselves frozen by the demand that as Christians they must communicate a Christian message in each and every painting. Many works by Christians will genuinely grow out of a Christian mentality and dependence upon divine grace, but still not be recognizable in any easy or immediate way as a Christian. This is the work which often puzzles those who want everything labelled.

The desire for a clear message, *in verbal terms* in a painting denies the potential of visual languages to open up imaginatively those areas which they are uniquely equipped to explore. This is not to erect a false conflict between the verbal and the visual. Verbal and visual understanding, though interwoven, do have areas of experience genuine to each, where one cannot replace the other. Not to recognize this is to see paintings as a kind of strange code unlocked by a verbal key. Then, the question 'What does it mean?' often hides a plea for a verbal substitute for the visual experience. No accumulation of essays will ever replace a Rembrandt self-portrait however helpful they are. No painting will ever replace Calvin's *Institutes of the Christian Religion*, though some paintings may help us to understand some aspects of his work.

In a certain sense, paintings have no 'meaning', if what is implied by the word is a simple one-to-one verbal explanation of each element in a painting. A visual statement often brings together a whole bundle of meanings and in that sense is meaningful. Some will be understood and intentional on the part of the painter, many will not. The painter uses what insights and ability he may possess to home in on the particular area of experience or reality to which he draws our attention. If he is successful, we will be drawn to those areas of understanding – provided, of course, that we share his cultural context and traditions. Yet here we face what appears to be a paradox. The painter's success can too easily be attributed to his control of the situation, as though he has encoded his message and we simply decode it. If, however, the success of the painter means that his perceptions and his ability to disclose them visually are in harmony with the way God's world really is, then that truth becomes beyond his control. The painting, as it truly opens our eyes, will have resonances and echoes which are unpremeditated, unsought and unrecognized by the artist himself. The situation God has made for us and placed us in is itself beyond our grasp. There are always new things that surprise us because of the narrowness of our perceptions. This is not to remove the value of the painting as a painting and suggest that a painting's value lies in what it means. Rather, I am attempting to suggest that the question of meaning in a visual statement becomes complex if we imagine we can replicate its meaningfulness in words.

In 1980 I completed a small wood engraving of a teddy bear. It is a rather conventional image, and, one would imagine, easy to understand. I still get asked, 'What does it mean?' though often the hidden question is 'Why did you want to make a print of a teddy bear?' or even 'Yes, but what is the *Christian* message?'

There is no explanation, at least in terms of 'Yes, it is a teddy bear but what it really means is x or y.' Even so, why did I do it? What was my intention? As my daughter's first teddy bear he had always interested me. His particular shape, clothes and expression are also visually interesting. Yet these things of themselves had not prompted a drawing. One evening, as the toys were being tidied away I noticed the bear lying in an awkward way like someone fallen in battle or leaping. The shapes were interesting to me so I drew attention to it by drawing. The drawing was in black and white because that seemed appropriate to the tonal contrasts, and I had no time to get out the paints.

I put the drawing away. A year later, having begun to make wood engravings, I came across the drawing. Being black and white it was readily transposed into a parallel set of drawing conventions. It also posed some good technical problems for a new wood-engraver. I made the print. By altering the tonal relationship between the beds and the floor the print became more sombre in feel. This and other changes in the visual language moved the image away from the original, particular moment without abandoning it. In this way, other more general implications may have filtered in. Little, if any, of this gets put into words before making begins or even in the act of making. The making, not the verbalization, seems to be the thinking.

The print potentially has many meanings. Some are brought about by the process itself which has its own expectations, history and a tradition of similar images. Others relate to the objects depicted which draw, magnet-like, other things towards them. 'It looks like someone fallen over.' The visual language employed, by its omissions as much as its inclusions, encourages or repels such attractions or associations. I do not feel it is necessary to have those or similar thoughts explained before one can enjoy the print. It still remains simply a nice teddy bear as well. I do not intend to give the impression that visual images are simply hooks on which you freely hang your own meanings or associations. The observer has to be able to participate imaginatively in the reconstruction of the state of affairs indicated by the visual language employed; but the meaning of the work arises out of, and is circumscribed by, the print itself rather than by something subsequently grafted on. Even those works which are intended to function as hooks for the observer's free association, indicate that use by their structure.

I have suggested that the idea of the painter as a 'unique-divinely-inspired individual with a prophetic message' is misguided, without denying either the real guidance of God in our daily work or the genuine power of a painting to move deeply, instruct or inspire.

I have questioned an approach to painting which reduces all such objects to being illustrations of world views, verbal concepts or message carriers, without implying that paintings are neutral with regard to content, or that they cannot be fruitfully discussed using words.

Our interest is not just in the queries we may have about the arts we question, but in alternative approaches which grow out of an understanding which is fed by the Christian faith. We turn then to the Bible for help, not because it contains a treatise on painting that is hidden away for the ingenious to discover, but because it provides the framework we need for out thoughts and deeds.

The Genesis account provides one key to our understanding of creation's structure and man's response. Initially this is more important than any consideration of how art and craft were sanctioned by God for use in conjunction with Old Testament worship. 'And the Lord God made all kinds of trees grow out of the ground – trees that were pleasing to the eye and good for food' (Gen. 2.9). We easily recognize the importance of 'good for food' but with that provision, we are given another one; the trees are pleasing to the eye. We need our attention drawn to the fact that the world, as made and pronounced good by God, had built into it a structure which man does not simply happen to find pleasing but which is deliberately made to harmonize with his own expectations of what is pleasing to the eye. Man is made with the ability to share the delight God has in his own creation. This is something external to man in that it is built into the trees just as the fruit is edible whether eaten or not. The trees have qualities which a human being will find pleasing to the eye.

Conversely, man himself is made to respond to these qualities. This involves more than a simple recognition of them. He has had to take and eat the fruit. He has to participate imaginatively in the visual appearance. We can too easily tend towards a kind of materialism which sees the world in terms of food value alone. This is not to imply that the 'pleasing-to-the-eye' kind of tree is more spiritual or morally uplifting than the 'good-for-food' tree. There is an overlap in these areas anyway. There is, though, a certain mentality which views the fallenness of the world as justification for growing vegetables in the garden because they can be eaten but not flowers because they have no 'use'.

The responsibilities to rule, replenish and subdue the earth which were given to Adam in the garden show us how we are to respond to creation. These responsibilities are clearly seen when God has Adam name the animals. In so naming them it becomes clear that none is suitable as the kind of helper God has in mind for Adam. This giving of names encapsulates many of man's activities as a shaper of the world. To name is to identify, catagorize and understand. To name also demands an imaginative response from Adam. God made the animals but Adam invented the names.

Sadly, as events showed, this is not man's only possible response. There is a framework within which a fruitful, unfolding, peaceful dominion and gentle stewardship of rotation has to take place. This involves trust in, and obedience to, the Creator. Outside this framework lies the result of disobedience and the temptation to usurp God himself. It was not the 'pleasing-to-the-eye' or the 'good-for-food' elements in the world which were evil, but rather, how these were transformed by the desire to be as God, and to take what had not yet been given.

Fallen man is still man. He still eats and is visually delighted but these activities are now distorted by the curse. Those things intended for our good we transform by sin into poison. Yet, the reality that men can be ruled by gluttony does not stop us from eating or enjoying food. The fact that aesthetics is for many a surrogate and illusory spiritual experience does not invalidate the real and potential good in that which is pleasing to the eye.

This is even more true when the world is viewed from the vantage point of the gospel in which we find a present and future redemption. The gospel provides the motives and the resources to challenge sin in all its manifestations, enabling us to reclaim God's gifts and the privilege to delight in them. It is difficult to assess exactly how the curse has changed creation itself, though it is clear that the 'pleasing-to-the-eye' of the trees is still there. Whether it is as clear and forceful now as it was then, who can tell? Whatever the answer, we have now to contend with the thorns and thistles; so in some sense creation itself works against us. Nevertheless, in spite of the aberrations of the curse we still recognize and appreciate those, 'pleasing-to-the-eye', moments in the created world. What then of man's artifacts in this context? Are they visually pleasing because they reflect or conform to that which makes us find creation visually pleasing?

The Old Testament concentrates on those artifacts whose manufacture God himself has instructed, namely the tabernacle and the temple. These include many complex and visually pleasing objects.[6] The materials used were visually attractive in themselves, as were the interpretations and representations of natural form. The other kind of objects which man makes in order to worship are, in the Old Testament, exposed as worthless and evil idols whether pleasant to look at or not.

We can learn much from the way in which the tabernacle and the temple were built and adorned, following as they do God's own instructions, without regarding them as some mystical blue-print for all subsequent architecture, art and craft. We have to remember that these artifacts are uniquely embedded in redemptive history as it unfolds in the life of God's chosen people. The life of Israel and the worship in the temple are essentially a pre-figuring, in physical terms, of what – for us in the New Covenant – is spiritually true in Christ. The ripping of the temple curtain from top to bottom at the death of Christ really *is* the end of the old way. We have no temple because we have no need of one. The church, as spiritual Israel, does not find its focus in any architecture or man-made artifact because these do not reflect its inner nature as the Body of Christ.

The New Testament is as silent about making paintings as it is about growing potatoes; but this does not mean that it has nothing to say to us. It maps out for us a way of life that is applicable whatever our individual gifts may be. Here we can find some starting points for our thinking about the activity of making paintings as this occurs in our own time and place.

Of abiding importance is the command that after loving God we must love our neighbour as ourselves. Here our own ego is shown its proper place. Quite simply, in God's service, our gifts and abilities are not given to us for our own enjoyment. True, there is a proper delight which we experience when our own actions seem right, proper or successful; but this finds its place as we become good neighbours.

Paul in his instructions to the young churches gives a description of the life-style which is implied by the gospel. This includes an attitude to daily work. He tells the Ephesians that the thief should not only stop stealing but that he 'must work, doing something useful with his own hands, that he may have something to share with those in need' (Eph.4:28). He urges Christians who are idle to 'settle down and earn the bread they eat' (2 Thess.3:12). To Titus he gives similar instructions: 'Our people must learn to devote themselves to doing what is good, in order that they may provide for daily necessities and not live unproductive lives' (Titus 3:14). This fits into the daily pattern when we realize that the phrase 'doing what is good' means 'honourable trades' or 'honest labour'. The Christian is to lead a fruitful life by doing honest work in order to provide daily necessities for himself, his family and for those in need.

Since these ground rules are applicable to all Christians, they have a bearing on the Christian painter. It is not enough to call one's work honest labour, fruitful as it may be, if it fails to provide for daily necessities. The painter who regards himself as a prophet and his work as being a special divine calling will be tempted to regard himself as a special case. He thinks his own gifts and work so important that surely he must be financially supported. As far as I can see Paul allows for no exceptions to his advice, bar that of being unable to do any work which will provide for daily needs. Such people are in need of help. To demand help when you do not need it is to take from those in genuine need.

This is not to minimize the problem. In our own society, at this time, given the priorities it manifests, the painter is financially in a weak position. This is especially true when there are many who desire any kind of honest labour but cannot find it; and very few artists manage to support themselves solely through the sale of paintings. This is not a new problem. The traditional solutions are still with us and while they may seem unfortunate they are not necessarily dishonourable. Other forms of employment have to be sought. These may utilize one's specific abilities in the arts, or they may make use of other skills.

The one calling which remains constant and unchanged by changing circumstances is the divine calling actually to behave as a Christian should. Potentially we each have many abilities. If I am a lawyer until I am forty years old there is no reason why I am forced to regard that as my calling for life. Other gifts develop with maturity as others may decline. To avoid misunderstanding let me stress that to do anything well involves hard work, dedication and self-sacrifice. If the painter should have a family they are hopefully supportive and can face such difficulties together, but this is no different from families in other walks of life. The painter who is a Christian is not free to abdicate from his responsibility to provide daily necessities or to be a good spouse or parent, because he imagines this stands in the way of his calling to be an artist.

However, those who enjoy and value the work of artists need to review their own attitudes. I have suggested that the painter, by his desire to behave responsibly and not burden the Church, may seek alternative employment. He seeks it, not because painting pictures is not work or honest labour but because in spite of the hard work involved it still does not provide daily necessities. One cannot demand that the painter devote all his energies to his painting in order to make something worthwhile without realizing the hard work and time involved. If your painter can only spend two days a week painting and the rest of his time in other ways providing daily necessities, it is too easy to condemn his faithfulness as lack of faith.

On the positive side there are many examples of individuals, who because of their high regard for someone else's particular giftedness, have taken steps to ensure that they can exercise those gifts. This is a difficult area with no easy solutions, especially when the individual's circumstances can vary so much.

Built into creation and ourselves as created are the desire and ability to find, make and delight in that which is pleasing to the eye. This is not only a passive activity, as though we enjoy what God has made as a vague background niceness which – though pretty at times – we can get along without. God insists that Adam acts in a way which orders and imaginatively transforms the world. This runs through all man's making and doing.

The two events which overlay this situation have already been referred to, namely the fall and redemption of man. These mould our circumstances, as man's sinful enslavement to God's good gifts finds liberation in man's redemption in Christ. We have no choice but to make every effort to dethrone the abstraction called Art wherever it presents itself as redeemer or lord – and in doing so we must call into question its priests, prophets and worshippers. To our relief, this does not overthrow art but potentially makes it free. All the power it possesses to enlarge our vision and heal some of our wounds is released in new and positive directions. Art is a good servant but a bad master.

To speak of painting as honest labour or an honourable trade has directed our attention to the craftsmanship or 'making' aspect of these gifts. We have also, indirectly, touched upon that other ingredient: the aesthetic dimension of our lives. Aesthetics, as a seperate branch of philosophical study, is relatively new. Its concern is what we find pleasing or beautiful whether that be in created things or men's making. It is not limited to visual languages but deals with that which pleases in other non-visual ways as well.

Theorists working from within the Reformed Christian tradition have attempted to identify norms which may help us to pin-point what is typical of aesthetic experience.

Writing as an art historian, Rookmaaker uses a term which has been translated as 'beautiful-fittingness'[7] to describe those harmonious qualities which we find aesthetically pleasing. Seerveld and Wolterstorff write with an interest in philosophical aesthetics. Seerveld[8], unhappy as a Christian with theories of beauty derived from pagan classicsm, suggests that a state or quality he calls 'allusiveness' or 'nuancefulness' provides a better starting point for descriptions of what is central to aesthetic experience. 'Peculiar to art is a parable character, a metaphoric intensity, an elusive play in its artifactual presentation of meanings apprehended.'[9]

Wolterstorff aims to clarify our understanding of the nature of aesthetic experience. Although pointing out that the disinterested contemplation of a work for its aesthetic value is only one possible use for a work of art, he does not suggest that such contemplation has no place within a Christian framework.[10] He identifies at least three factors[11] which contribute to our ascribing aesthetic merit to an object or work. The work will be unified in character, although there are many ways of making a unity. The work will be to some degree internally rich, although there are many types of complexity. The work will also be 'fitting'. Wolterstorff describes the artist as a worker in 'fittingness'. He describes fittingness as similarity across modalities.[12] When we say that sugar is sweet we mean it literally in the sense that we can taste its sweetness. When we say that a piece of music is sweet or a painting sour we are finding similarities across modalities.

There will continue to be much discussion at a theoretical level about the precise nature of aesthetics and aesthetic experience. These researches and insights are, of course, interesting to the painter, and even though I shall be emphasizing the centrality of aesthetic experience, paintings have non-aesthetic implications. One could even say that some insights into these non-aesthetic areas are only mediated to us via aesthetic experience. While it is sometimes helpful to be aware of work of a theoretical nature in aesthetic theory, aesthetic theory cannot be regarded as a blueprint, or set of verbal instructions, on the making of paintings.

This aesthetic dimension, however, makes itself felt in all the things that we make.

Imagine that when driving the car you come across a man-made object by the side of the road and as you approach you begin to contemplate its aesthetic qualities. There is something pleasing about the three circles of coloured glass. Meanwhile, the person next to you is shouting 'Stop! Stop! It's on red!'

The traffic light does have an aesthetic aspect as an object. Its visual structure and design may be interesting but in this context these qualities serve a non-aesthetic function. If (in this context) they draw attention to themselves as primarily a source of aesthetic contemplation they fail in their intended use. Conversely, if the importance of the aesthetic dimension is totally ignored, we might never notice them – causing them to fail in another way. Here then the aesthetic element, though positively present, serves the simple end of bearing the messages, 'stop', 'take care' or 'go'.

The development of the London Tube map provides another interesting example. When Beck invented this useful stylization of the underground railway system in the 1930s, his ideas grew from a simple sketch on the back of an envelope. Today, in spite of subsequent revisions, the basic concept is relatively unchanged. The revisions have taken the form of manipulations of the component parts in an attempt to achieve clarity and visual harmony. Circles were found to be preferable to diamonds as a symbol for interchange stations and certain colour combinations, for example, better than others. Here we perhaps see the interplay between what Rook-maaker calls the 'iconic' and 'aesthetic' elements. He uses the word iconic to refer to the fact that 'we can express something by means of lines, colours and three-dimensional forms – in a similar way to what happens in language by means of sounds.'[13] He argues that there are many image-languages possible, and that their success lies in the clarity with which the structure of things must be represented.

The Underground map is a good example of a case where verbal language fails but an image-language is successful. It can, clearly and without ambiguity, direct our attention to that aspect of the Underground system which as passengers we need to understand. It is so specific in its design that if fails if used for any other purpose.

Beck's first design was iconically clear, as were each of the subsequent revisions. It was attention to the aesthetic element as supportive of that clarity which influenced decisions with respect to revision. Not only do the colours act iconically as they clearly delineate the different routes; their choice contributes to the overall harmony and this involves aesthetic decisions.

While the purpose of visual language, in so far as it is iconic, is not always aesthetic disclosure or expansion there will always be a supportive aesthetic element. This is true also of verbal language. One does not expect a motor car manual to be rich in metaphor or 'allusiveness'; yet if no regard at all is given to literary aesthetics, its verbal style might make reading it unpleasant.

When we make paintings the aesthetic element overlays, and is built upon, the iconic or the fact that we can depict something by visual means. I may collect old traffic lights or the various editions of the Tube maps because I like them – but this use is subsequent to their intended function.

The original drawings for the Tube map were made with the limitations of the final commercial printing process in mind. The skill lies in producing artwork which anticipates the changes involved and positively utilizes the particular qualities of the reproductive process. It is possible that original artwork which is made specifically for reproduction will look as though it lacks visual harmony, because it relies on the printing process itself to provide the integration and to be the unifying factor.

When the intended use of a painting is not as artwork for reproduction the reverse is true. One can only really experience a painting by first hand experience. This is not to mystify paintings as strange precious objects, but to concede quite simply that the painting has a potential richness, aesthetic subtlety and complexity which cannot be transposed. To change, for example, the green of the District Line and make it a bit more blue or yellow, although altering the appearance of the map, will not impair its function provided the District Line remains distinct. To reproduce a painting and change its colours, tonality, its surface quality, its scale and context is to see a shadow of the actual painting. I was familiar with Vermeer's painting *The Milkmaid* in reproduction. This meant I had no problem identifying the image when I saw it in the gallery. I was left completely unprepared for the richness of the encounter. To look at the painting was a deeply moving experience, because the reproduction only vaguely hinted at the aesthetic power of the work.

So our lives are interwoven with aesthetic moments which at certain times, in certain places and in certain objects become more pronounced. In a painting this aesthetic element bubbles and rises to the surface as the main object and integrating agent by which our understanding is enlarged and our insights refreshed. To suggest that the function of a painting is aesthetic is not to advocate a kind of formal aestheticism or 'art for art's sake'. The reaction was perhaps understandable in a society where paintings have been respected for their moral, religious, political or financial value and judged by these standards, while the aesthetic aspect is undervalued or ignored.

The solution does not lie in a search for 'pure aesthetic experience'. To make the aesthetic function central in a painting is not to isolate it or remove it from contact with the environment in which it asserts itself. The aesthetic element in other areas of life, plays its part if you like, as a servant. In a painting the aesthetic element becomes central and is itself served. Yet even with the support of (for example) moral values, the painting will succeed or fail as it is measured against aesthetic criteria.

This is why we are often faced with the confusing problem of a painting which is extremely effective as a painting whose supportive and implicit morality for example is totally offensive. If we wish to retain our moral stance, we are forced to that extent into uncertainty or rejection in spite of aesthetic success. On the other hand, who gives a second glance at a morally upright but aesthetically inept painting? In spite of our sympathy with its supportive moral framework, if we wish to retain our aesthetic integrity we do not waste too much of our time on the painting.

Rookmaaker, in referring to John Ruskin's views, says this:

> As a result of the creative activity of man a work of art will have to appeal to man as a totality, it will have to possess a fulness and riches exactly consisting in the close relationship between the iconic element representing reality and the aesthetic element constituting the beauty of the work of art.[14]

We do not suspend the rest of our humanity with its interwoven complex of beliefs and convictions in order to have a pure aesthetic experience when we are confronted with a painting, but we must recognize that first and foremost it is an aesthetic or 'painterly' experience. This aesthetic experience is thrown into relief, not because it disowns and separates itself from the rest of human experience but because it asserts its own centrality, value and importance within that context.

Seerveld argues that increasing cultural differentiation in society makes it possible for us to value paintings for their painterliness.[15] Wolterstorff also shows how alongside the development of aesthetics as a separate discipline certain works of art come to be valued for, and specifically made as, objects of detached aesthetic contemplation.[16] It is this group of objects and events that he would describe as 'fine art'. He also warns us that not all visual images are made with this intention. There are other forms of visual depiction where though the aesthetic element plays a large and conspicuous role, in the final analysis it is guided by other considerations. One has only to think of much of the visual imagery associated with advertising.

In a similar way, not all paintings can be said to have the aesthetic function as central. Making paintings does have a therapeutic or healing aspect for the painter. To what extent the therapy relates to making as such, or is specifically associated with aesthetic decisions, I am not sure. It can be so strong that some have made this the central function of all art, regarding it as *the* healer of individuals and society. In our broken situation, all work brings with it the equivalent problems of the gardener's thorns and thistles. In that sense things are against us. If a patient begins to paint for therapeutic purposes then the declared intention of the activity is therapeutic. If aesthetic goals take the patient into areas where the painting ceases to aid therapy, then it fails. After a certain point the therapeutic element is overlaid by non-therapeutic aesthetic demands.

A similar situation may occur when paintings are made as a form of relaxation. Painting often is a pleasurable activity. Painters who paint for relaxation often work very hard indeed, but as long as the declared intention is relaxation, then the moment the painting takes them into the kind of anxieties and perplexities which arise in what we call 'work' then they will stop painting. Paintings produced for the relaxation of the painter tend to rely heavily, no matter how cleverly, on visual clichés. (These of course are generalizations. What begins as therapy or relaxation might easily continue into something else.)

In speaking of painting in this way I am not seeking to perpetuate the myth of high and low art. It is not true that activities like painting are high, lofty and morally superior to designing pleasing and successful railway maps. Each is important in its own context, fulfilling its own particular function. Each can be done, with integrity, in a way which honours God and serves neighbours. This is neither to deny that often a well-designed chair, say, may give more aesthetic pleasure than an ill-conceived painting.

However, our attempts to remove painting from the idolatrous pedestal it has had built for it are not helped by claiming that there is no difference between designing a margarine wrapper and painting a portrait. No matter how pleasing, well-designed, popular or useful a margarine wrapper may be, it does not have – or need – the same complexity or potential to enlarge those parts of our being which are moved by, say, a Rembrandt self-portrait. To place the brilliantly-designed wrapper alongside a terrible painting would not make the wrapper possess the potential to provide those disclosures possible in the painting. This is not true even when, later, the wrapper may come to be valued as a pleasing object in itself.

Though we might reject the idea of high and low art, the terms fine and applied art (once the associations with high and low are removed) still seem useful. They at least distinguish between those objects or events whose function in our society is aesthetic, from those with other functions. This chapter has been concerned with that kind of painting the intention of which is primarily aesthetic disclosure. We must be careful, though, not to tie down the 'pleasing-to-the-eye' aspect of reality by easily identifying it with theories of beauty. Paintings which by such standards might not be regarded as strictly beautiful may nevertheless possess fittingness, inner harmony or allusive qualities which are still 'pleasing-to-the-eye'.

It is one thing to theorize about paintings and another to actually paint. What form should my visual language take? How does it relate to the visual traditions one inherits? How do I give form to that which I imagine is possible? How do I identify the content of my work? It should come as no surprise that the answer to these and similar questions can only be found by working and actually using the language. Gere Veith Jr for example, tries to solve the problem of form and content by making one of no consequence. He says: 'Questions of form are basically indifferent. Christians are free to pursue any formal mode of art they find congenial.'[17] He then gives examples of photo-realism, expressionism and abstraction.

In trying to understand how a painting works these terms might be useful up to a certain point. When I paint this distinction seems irrelevant because it fails to account for the realities involved. If we take form and content too literally, it becomes easy to identify content with 'ideas' and form as any convenient vehicle to carry them; just as a railway wagon may carry logs one day and bricks the next without any change in its own appearance. Do I have a good idea and then visit the supermarket of available styles, pick a nice contemporary-looking form, and then get to work?

To have this distinction in mind while making a painting may well work against the very activity of painting. I certainly come to a painting with preconceptions of one kind or another. They may relate to the content side of the coin or I may want to make a particular kind of painting and be thinking about the formal means to adopt. Usually both are involved. Such preconceptions may be vague and unrecognized or carefully considered. In the event, they are only proved to have value if they can survive the painting process and so demonstrate their visual worth. As I make the marks and grapple with a growing physical object I often discover what interests me or recognize the content. In struggling to make something known, I may discover the kinds of visual language I need. The painting seems to have a life of its own because the process is fed from many sources some of which, because of their nature, are beyond the control of the artist.

The language I use as I write is common property to whoever can read and understand it. When the language is used for its aesthetic value the form and content are bound together. It can be used in a way in which, for example, not only is the content nasty or joyful in some way but the formal properties of the language are equally disturbing or exhilarating. We cannot regard form as simply a matter of indifference, because when that particular form of language is used again it will still retain some of its nastiness or joy. This fact, the interplay and interdependence of what we call form and content, gives added variety and complexity as well as providing a pitfall for the unwary. It is possible by accident or design to allow a joyful content to be confused and lost by using a form that is suited to other ends. One can also disguise an otherwise disturbing or destructive content by clothing it in sweetness and light. The variations seem endless. The thing we need to remember is that the form is as important and value-laden as any content.

We must not forget the importance of context, both the 'internal' context established by the work which identifies its genre and range of expectations, and the external context of time and place. The word 'the' or a single note of music, as they exist outside of such a contextual framework, are not 'good' or 'bad'. However, as they take their own place and become a piece of music or literature, then form and content are married. Form and content will tend to draw attention to themselves as separate entities when, for whatever reason, the work is somehow inappropriate or not fitting.

Christ warns us that in our use of language there is no such thing as the casual word. All words will have to be accounted for. Is it too speculative to believe that we ought to be equally serious in our use of visual language? In a real way a painting's form unlocks its content. If we do regard form as a matter of indifference we could easily find ourselves painting pictures which we sincerely believe to be saying one thing while the work because of its form is saying something quite different. Some forms of visual language are intended to be vile and offensive, trivial or degrading. Yet others are designed to initiate us into a surrogate spirituality. It is inconceivable, for example, to think of changing any of the formal properties of a Francis Bacon painting while leaving the content of the work intact. It is equally impossible to imagine how one could regard the form in a Francis Bacon as a matter of indifference and try to make use of it to project a Christian view of man. This is true even if one were painting the blacker side of human nature. Man's sin, no matter how dehumanizing, does not make him any less human nor does it occur outside the realm of mercy. The simple power of successful painting can disarm us. The often dazzling appeal of what presents itself as contemporary relevance and is ardently promoted as such can instill in us that fear of being on the outside of the inner circle.

The answer does not lie in absolute rejection of all the paintings of which we disapprove. No one can make something which is totally negative. Even the most destructive work will depend at some point on the structures which it denies. Not every mark or formal invention of Bacon's is necessarily negative as such. There may be moments of truth in that which seems totally despicable. It will take a certain kind of insight to pick through the debris in order to see if any of these moments can be salvaged. They will still need a new visual context in which to grow.

I am not implying that there is for the Christian a single form of visual language which can be identified as the 'Christian' way. In our criticism and evaluation of paintings it is all too easy to give the impression that there is only one kind of painting to which all must aspire. This mistake is more often made by those who set too much store by aesthetic experience and so disperse into competing cults, each claiming to have the authentic fragment of the True Painting. In such situations the quality of a work can be lost sight of. All that matters for them is whether or not it belongs to the right camp.

On the other hand painting is not a neutral activity. We cannot argue that it is simply a natural gift which operates by its own laws outside the context of Christian faith. This would reintroduce that old false split between nature and grace. We can talk about painting, whoever does it, in a normative rather than neutral sense. When a car is running well it does not draw attention to itself, it simply does what it has been designed to do. Many of the daily activities we take part in as Christians are like that. Our actions and attitudes grow implicitly out of the gospel. It is only the brokenness of the situation which often draws attention to normative behaviour. To love one's wife if the majority despise theirs is in that context to have the appearance of abnormality while in actual fact being normal.

This distortion of normality may mean that we have to struggle to reclaim our normality in Christ. The 'pleasing-to-the-eye' element of creation is not our invention. We can expect it to have inherent norms and principles which guide and direct its most fruitful use. These we discover as we work within God's structured world. The visual languages developed and developing in response to these norms are rich and varied. In the same way that not all our actions, even though they are built on the gospel, shout from the roof tops 'Look! This is a Christian act', so not all paintings will be explicit in their underlying faith. Much of our work as Christians will implicitly grow out of the gospel without drawing overt attention to that fact.

The gospel in fact enlarges our sphere of operations because it removes so many hindrances. It clears away from us all the dead wood of pride, false ambition and self-seeking. These are the things which would consume us and absorb our time and energy. We are forced even to reject that old maxim, so beloved by painters, that above all we have to be 'true to ourselves'. It is only in being true to God that we can ever hope to be honest about ourselves. Then we often discover that it would show no love to our neighbour to bludgeon him over the head with our wickedness, under the deceptive guise of our professed artistic integrity.

We have to understand that there are many kinds of painting because of the richness and complexity of our situation. Visual language itself is not static. Of necessity we work within a particular tradition. Tradition of itself is not negative. More often than not, it provides the continuity and mind-set from which that which is remarkable springs. Even the effectiveness of those who wish to destroy all structures and traditions can only be felt in the context of what is destroyed.

Any visual tradition will have its clichés and outworn modes. What once gave form to a new insight, or reinstated a lost value, itself loses value by constant repetition. The challenge is to find ways to rescue the values we do not want to see lost. Kim Kempshall, in a paper given to postgraduate Fine Art students, says: 'Truly original work will then spring out of necessity when existing language-forms prove inadequate to embody emergent new ideas and fresh insights.'[18]

As we explore our freedom as painters, we will discover that it is not an absolute freedom but one which has true bounds. These are not easily or necessarily codified for the artist, although the boundaries can be recognized as they are approached or crossed. Giving visual expression, for example, to an exploration of the inner world of one's subjective states may be legitimate; but it may reach a point where it becomes gross self-obsession.

There are varieties of gift and insight on the part of the painters themselves. It is one thing to recognize one's potential freedoms but quite another to realize these in a tangible form. Here the gospel provides us with a particular freedom. To realize that I am not Rembrandt does not destroy my integrity as a painter. A painting can be simple or conventional in visual language terms without being trivial or worthless.

This is not an argument for the elevation of the mediocre. There are great men and women who are able to be innovative or extend the visual language in dramatic ways but in the nature of the case they are exceptions rather than the rule. Even so, it has often been the unrecognized and minor imaginative achievements of less gifted artists which have provided the springboard and framework for the exceptional achievements of the great painters.

Each painter has to discover the actual bounds of his own gift-edness. He will then be able to extend and use his gifts as best he can. In so doing it is often the case that such gifts can be stretched further than imagined. Better this, than the bitter self-condemnation many artists inflict upon themselves when they discover that they are not one of art history's chosen few. Kim Kempshall again draws our attention to a similar problem when speaking of the pressures faced by painters: 'By thrusting narcissistic self-consciousness upon the painter and pressing for overt evidence of "originality" the very qualities which make an artist's work authentic may be stifled.'[19]

The different personalities we have been given will in turn give rise to different kinds of painting. We know that paintings are not necessarily autobiographical. One can paint a melancholy painting without being melancholic while painting it. Nevertheless, it should not surprise us that a painting betrays the personal biases or traits of the painter.

There are also many modes of painting. The internal demands for a state of completion or resolution in any painting depend upon the set of expectations provided by the painter in the work. So, too, the medium will assert its own presence and demands. A water-colour painting will have included, in the criteria by which it is judged a success or failure, observations which relate to the history, use, innovations and potential of watercolour itself.

Paintings are destined for a multiplicity of contexts. It is one thing to make a painting for a domestic interior, another to make one for a public space and another to make one as a contribution to a specialized aesthetic debate. There are also different audiences. As we, as painters, attempt to be of service to our fellow human beings it may be that our gifts and insights are of more use and value to some than others. In some cases this may be a small circle of friends, in others a much larger audience. If we choose to immerse ourselves in some obscure aesthetic problem, the solution of which will only be recognized and appreciated by those with a similar education and specialist interest then – no matter how worthwhile our efforts are – we are in no position to complain that we have no popular audience. Similarly, if we choose to adopt those simplifications which will become necessary in order to work for a wider audience, we have also to accept the limits this imposes on the potential subtlety or complexity of our work. Having said that, we know that good paintings are able to retain their integrity and transcend the vicissitudes of particular times and places.

We should expect to find that the framework of the gospel, and the mentality which grows from it, provides for many and varied examples of painting. The fact that the gospel has its prohibitions implies that there are ways of painting, types of subject matter and forms of visual language contrary to that gospel. What it does *not* imply is that only one kind of painting which is easily tagged as 'Christian' is what remains. For the Christian who is trying to be faithful in his work, in one sense, that faith will be always present but not always easily or immediately recognized. Sometimes it will be implicit like the hidden underground river from which, though unseen, we draw our strength. In other works it may rush like a torrent on the surface for all to see. Our hope would be that whatever it is, it is characterized by that humility which is appropriate to those who know God's grace. It may have strength without agression or humour without mockery. It may be gentle without being weak and pointed but not barbed. It may be a simple painting working with sensitivity well within the conventions of its own tradition. It may be a work which is ambitious as it questions traditional boundaries in search of newer insights.

In the final analysis we cannot truly understand what God gave us when he made painting – something that people can do in response to what he has made – if we deny that a painting's value is mediated to us in a physical sensuous form. Indeed, its very value lies in the reality that is the painterliness of painting to which we respond.

When we enter into a landscape painting[20] we can be moved and intrigued by the world the painter projects in a way that is quite unlike our response to the landscape itself even if that is an aesthetic one. This is because we move in a landscape that has been imaginatively transformed by the painter. We will recognize those points where it accords with our own experience of landscape, and appreciate those reassurances. We may also be exposed to those new experiences the painter has disclosed, which challenge and enlarge our assumptions. We can enjoy the interplay in the painting with a tradition of similar expectations and perceptions. We can become immersed in the inventiveness of the formal language as the shapes, forms and colours are themselves as they lie on a flat surface and yet become other things as well. We delight in the moment of completeness as what seem disparate elements come together into a complex whole.

It is the very power of painting which has led people to believe that it can offer more than it does in terms of ultimate experiences.

This should not cause us, in over-reaction, to deny the reality of its power for good. It is something of this danger that Wolterstorff has in mind when he says:

> The abhorrence of the physical and the sensory is so deeply ingrained in Western Christendom that there will be those who agree that aesthetic delight is legitimate while continuing to believe that delight in the words or the paint or the sounds is to be scorned devoting all their attention to the scene or story.

He goes on to say, 'So it can be said emphatically: This world of colours and textures and shapes and sounds is good for us, good for us in many ways, good also in that it provides us with refreshing delight.'[21] This is not to reduce paintings to pleasant patterns, but to focus on the total impact of painting.

When working, the painter is usually alone and can become rather isolated. Too often a combination of circumstances and education make the painter jealously individualistic. Peter Fuller suggests that 'Good art can only be realized when a creative individual encounters a living tradition with deep tendrils in communal life.'[22] We need to identify our living tradition. It will have to be large enough to value and incorporate innovation. At the same time we need to cultivate our communal Christian experience of the visual arts. Then we shall value paintings and those who can make them for us.

To abondon this area altogether is to deny the goodness and wisdom of God in making for us that which is pleasing to the eye. To embrace these gifts of God, in the setting of the fall and redemption of mankind, is to enter into that spiritual battle with its present mingling of joy and tears. The Christian painter needs to take this work seriously as honest labour which plays its part in unfolding the potential of creation in service to Christ and one's neighbour.

Notes

1. C. S. Lewis, 'Good work and Good works', *Screwtape Proposes a Toast*, Glasgow, 1977 p. 118.
2. E. Kris and O. Kurz, *Legend, Myth and Magic in the Image of the Artist*, Yale University Press, London, 1979, p. 48.

3. H. R. Rookmaaker, 'The Artist as a Prophet', *Art and the Public Today*, Huemoz-sur-Ollon, 1968.

4. R. Ellmann and C. Fiedelson, eds., *The Modern Tradition*, Oxford, 1965, pp. 195, 197.

5. N. Wolterstorff, *Art in Action*, Mi, Grand Rapids, 1980, p. 89.

6. F. A. Schaeffer, *Art and the Bible*, London, 1973.

7. C. Seerveld, *Rainbows for the Fallen World*, Toronto, 1980, p.122.

8. Ibid., chap. 4, 'Modal Aesthetic Theory, Prelim Questions', p. 104ff.

9. Ibid, p. 27.

10. Op. cit., 'Norms in Art', p.156ff.

11. Ibid, p. 163ff.

12. Ibid., 'The given with which the Artist works', p. 91.

13. H. R. Rookmaaker, *Synthetist Art Theories*, Amsterdam, 1959, pp. 204, 205.

14. Ibid., p. 217.

15. Op. cit., Chap. 6, 'Modern Art and the Birth of a Christian Culture', p. 156.

16. Op. cit., pp. 36–9.

17. C. E. Veith, Jr., *The Gift of Art*, Downers Grove, Ill, 1983, p. 59.

18. K. Kempshall, 'Objective Painting', unpublished notes for postgraduate painting students, Birmingham Polytechnic, 1979.

19. Ibid.

20. Here I had in mind a landscape by Kim Kempshall in the exhibition of paintings at the London Institute for Contemporary Christianity in 1985.

21. Op. cit., p. 82.

22. P. Fuller, *Aesthetics after Modernism*, London, 1983, pp. 36, 37.

Other Marshall Pickering Paperbacks

EYES THAT SEE: The Spiritual Gift of Discernment

Douglas McBain

The first of a new series, Renewal Issues in the Church, which examines the effects of charismatic renewal on corporate church life and individual Christian experience from a biblical perspective.

Douglas McBain, a leading figure in renewal first in the Baptist Church and now on a wider basis, provides a comprehensive and thorough scripture-based guide to the gift of discernment; which, with the resurgence of emphasis on signs and wonders, healing and deliverance, is 'the most necessary gift for the present day church'.

ISSUES FACING CHRISTIANS TODAY

John Stott

A major appraisal of contemporary social, moral, sexual and global issues, combined with one man's attempt to think 'Christianly' on this broad spectrum of complex questions, make ISSUES FACING CHRISTIANS TODAY a *best-seller*.

'This is powerful stuff. Highly contemporary . . . awkwardly personal . . . thoroughly biblical.'   *Baptist Times*

'A valuable resource for Christians responding to the huge needs to seek the renewal of society.'   *Buzz*

'It stands alone as a scholarly, scriptural and profoundly well-argued and researched authority on many of the most perplexing and intractable problems of the present day.'   *Renewal*

TWO MILLION SILENT KILLINGS: the Truth about Abortion

Dr Margaret White

Essential, informed reading for all Christians on this critical contemporary issue; likely to engender wholehearted and healthy controversy.

GP Margaret White exposes the deliberate attempt to confuse the public over the issue of abortion by the use of euphemistic language and the minimizing of its harmful side-effects. She traces the history of abortion from legal, medical and religious perspectives, describes the clinical methods used to terminate pregnancies, and answers the various arguments put forward by the pro-abortionists in terms of God's basic rules for life. At the heart of these is the Creator's desire for his creation's health, stability and well-being. Dr White demonstrates that the extent of the damaging effects of abortion on women and society is one of today's best-kept secrets.

THE GOSPEL COMMUNITY

John Tiller

An important and timely call to the established churches to rediscover the distinctive life of the Spirit and to become true 'gospel communities' – attractive, authoritative and relevant.

Neither the experience of renewal nor nationwide evangelistic missions resulted in a mass return to the churches. Instead, the house church seems to promise a better future for Christianity. Can revival still come through the established churches? John Tiller, Chancellor and Canon Residentiary of Hereford Cathedral, looks at Jesus' radical definitions of the temple, priesthood and sacrifice, and outlines the style of leadership which will enable the church to become again a 'living temple'. A critical book practically showing the way ahead for the established church.

CHOICES . . . CHANGES

Joni Eareckson Tada

Joni has inspired millions with her courage and faith in dealing with her quadriplegia. In her third book, she writes revealingly of her life, her ministry and her marriage. 'I've sat in on bridal showers for so many others; it seems odd that it should be my turn. In my wheelchair with its dusty gears and squeaky belts, I seem slightly out of place among the delicately wrapped gifts and dainty finger sandwiches.'

This warm, honest, sometimes funny and often poignant autobiography shows us vividly that though life is full of changes – wanted and unwanted – God uses each one of them to make us more like Him. Illustrated.

THE INFINITE GUARANTEE: A Meditation on the Last Words from the Cross

Andrew Cruickshank

A profound and thoughtful series of reflections on Jesus' seven sayings from the Cross by one of TV's most familiar and favourite actors. Andrew Cruickshank's deeply challenging study provides ideal devotional reading material, which encourages us to establish their significance of Jesus' words for us today.

'. . . a very remarkable book . . . quite outstanding. It demands to be read, re-read and read again. I can only describe it as *a little masterpiece . . .*'
Rev Dr William Neil